GUIDE TO  R

LIFESTYLE 2022

VOLUME ONE

MO2VATE Magazine

By Sharon Brown

Published by The Book Chief Publishing House 2022
(a trading name under Lydian Group Ltd)
Suite 2A, Blackthorn House, St Paul's Square, Birmingham, B3 1RL
www.thebookchief.com

British Library Cataloguing in Publication Date: A catalogue record for this
book is available from the British Library.

Book Cover Design: Deearo Marketing
Editor / Proof-reader: Laura Billingham
Coordinator: Nicola Matthews
Proof-reader / Typesetter / Publisher: Sharon Brown

THE BOOK CHIEF®

IGNITE YOUR WRITING

Table of Contents

FOREWORD

By Leanne Hawker

Living a healthy lifestyle can seem like an uphill struggle in today's world. Everyone has an opinion; everyone is an expert, and there are temptations and conflicting advice at every turn.

As a young girl, I had always wanted to write a book; journalism was the career I longed for, but like many things in life, we often find ourselves on another path, and our childhood ambitions fly out of the window. Finding Mo2vate magazine was like opportunity knocking, a chance to put my words out there, and maybe someone would read them.

I often let opportunities pass me by, overthinking to the point of standstill, but for some reason, I decided to go for it submitting my first article and crossing my fingers! I was thrilled to receive the email letting me know that my article had been chosen to be featured in the next edition of Mo2vate magazine.

I received some lovely feedback which helped my confidence, and then finding out I had also made centre spread was amazing! It was like a validation of a skill set that I had forgotten about, left unnurtured and filed away.

When you subscribe to Mo2vate magazine, you can see the quality and knowledge of the other contributors and the magazine is full of articles on mindset, business and health to name a few.

Suddenly, my inspiration to write came flooding back. I have had another article feature in Mo2vate and am currently working on my third. Not only that, but the opportunities keep coming, and one of those is having the opportunity to co-author this book with many other outstanding Mo2vate contributors.

In this book, you will find a wealth of knowledge on living a healthy lifestyle, with something to suit everyone. Advice from experts in the field of health and wellness who hope to inspire you to take that next step on your journey and find simple, uncomplicated answers.

As Gandhi said, "It is health that is real wealth and not pieces of gold and silver."

INTRODUCTION

Thank you for purchasing a copy of this book.

The Authors within this book have chosen to collaborate to provide a guide to various areas within health and wellness. All opinions and writing is their own.

This book has been brought together through MO2VATE Magazine and the catalyst for this was the bonus HEALTH issue which was published in July 2021.

All health article writers from June 2020 were asked if they wanted to take part in this publication and the result is this fantastic 17 chapter jam packed book full of amazing knowledge-based experience on how to live a healthier life.

We hope you enjoy.

CHAPTER 1

Staying healthy and beautiful as you age

By Alicja Son

Beauty can be defined in different ways; it's personal to each one of us; we give meaning to beauty.

I was sitting on the bench at the park, sipping freshly ground coffee from a pop-up independent organic café in Kensington Park near the Diana Memorial Playground, which I loved spending time by. The sun gently warmed my skin, a little cool air breeze, making me feel alert and at ease, birds chirping in the distance. It all felt idyllic, watching my daughter play on slides, climbing equipment, sandpit, laughing, and seeing her living in the present moment of pure joy and discovery.

I looked around and saw so many of the mothers with their children; some looked good and glamorous for their age; some were busy on their phones, a few were playing with their little ones, while others looked tired, stressed, or worn down. I started to wonder, what do they do to stay young-looking? How do we keep our vitality, strength, and mobility as we age?

As I watched people come by me on their way out of the park, there was a woman in her late 40s who had such a sparkle about her, such energy, her skin looked flawless, it made me want to know more about how she achieved it. So, when she was passing by and looking to sit on another bench to watch her little one, I turned around and said hello, then asked if we could speak for just a moment because I wanted to ask what her secret was to staying youthful? She smiled warmly at me but seemed reluctant to talk. As if she saw me as a threat in the beauty department, I was dead in the water before I even had my research going.

I explained to her that it wasn't about being competitive, but rather just curiosity on my part because her skin looked great, and she had a vibrancy, a glow about her that made me wonder what her secrets were.

She then asked if I had a few minutes because she would love to talk to me about what she does.

I looked around and saw that my daughter was just fine playing with the other children, so we agreed to sit on the bench where there were no distractions. We introduced ourselves, and she said to call her Emma.

I told her that I knew she might not want to reveal all her secrets, but if there was anything she could give me, it would be greatly appreciated because I had tried everything already, and my skin is far from glowing, so is my hair and nails. She empathised and said that I should not feel bad because that is what most women say when they find out her secret. They try creams and all sorts.

Emma said that she knew if I tried what she did, it would work for not only me but also many other women and men on my health blog because I shared with her that I love sharing tips on anything health related. I help people start making progress and changes, leading a healthier, more fulfilling lifestyle. I then asked again what the secret was that made her skin look so fantastic!

Emma leaned in close to me, smiled, and whispered in my ear, "I drink natural supplements, vitamins, and minerals, enzymes, every day, no excuses."

"What?!" I said.

She pulled back, looked at me, and calmly repeated, "Every day I drink natural supplements, you know multi-nutrients, collagen, chlorophyllin, herbs, providing my body with what it needs, every single day.

It is the secret to staying looking young, plus a little stretch here and there, walking, laughing with friends, drinking water, ah... don't forget to add moisture to your skin and give yourself time to just breathe. Enjoy your life darling! Are you against this idea?"

It took a second for it to soak into my brain, but once it did, I was like a kid in the pick n mix aisle! I am not sure what I expected the answer to be. I was most surprised there was no expensive price tag or creams mentioned. Of course! So simple! Consistency, the right nutrition, synergy, combine my good habits, breathe, stick to it, hey-presto! Easier said than done.

Emma responded: That's right. The rest is up to you, and she shared the secret of what supplements she used and showed me some of her pictures from a year or more ago from her phone picture gallery. The change in her skin appearance, hair, nails...wow! More importantly, she shared the incremental change in her as she continued her health journey.

Minerals and vitamins, amino acids, enzymes may be invisible to the naked eye, but they are what powers our cells, makes our body work optimally. Let's just take the mineral magnesium as an example.

Did you know that our body uses magnesium in about 300 biochemical reactions every single day? Magnesium is fundamental to producing cellular energy, helps to maintain the nervous system and muscle and bone function, supports the immune system, and keeps the heart beat at a steady pace; it's even needed to support blood glucose levels.

Moving on in time, since using natural supplements and nutrients alongside my healthier lifestyle hacks, I noticed better alertness, my hair getting stronger, ridges on nails disappearing, fewer colds, headaches, my immune system seemed to have a boost. Looking forward to waking up in the morning to a refreshing shower, a glass of water with chlorophyllin, and starting my day with a welcoming sun salutation or meditative state.

How do you know how to supplement correctly and integrate into your life?

Off I went to a local drug store to see what was on offer. I did internet research, spoke to a few more people in the health industry and listened to blogs and podcasts.

I read a few pub-med studies and books about trials and tests, and by the time I'd read a few pages, I was lost for words; there is so much confusion out there, so many differentiating views.

Do I buy these synthetic pills or their natural counterparts, or do I just eat healthily, or should I invest in these lush creams and conditioners that promise it all? I learned from doing the research that the quality of products varies greatly, so read what you buy, avoid bulking agents, binders, emulsifiers, artificial flavours, and synthetic colouring. Understand how the supplement is preserved for freshness, especially when buying prebiotics, probiotics, symbiotics. Cross-reference what you read for accuracy. So, if supplementation works, why doesn't everybody do this?

Well, many of us supplement, but probably not in the way we ought to. I have learned on my skin that supplementation works, but not any supplementation, a good quality natural supplement with the right synergy. We are speaking about functional foods, well balanced healthy diet, herbs and spices. The interaction between the individual minerals, vitamins and enzymes, and foods is what makes absorption possible. Also, if you want to look after your skin from the inside and out, there are a few that you can apply topically to support your skin. Geothermal, natural hot springs are amazing for this, but you can also make your own face mask, body scrub, even salve.

And that, ladies and gentleman, is how this secret stayed no more. I am about to share it more, so read on.

The irony is you stare at the answers every single day. Yes, that banana going black in the fruit bowl, that water with a bit of lemon and mint that you haven't drunk fully, or a mineral water bottle that you meant to drink during your lunch break, that sourdough bread drying in the breadbasket - they all have the natural biological background which synthetic ones often lack.

The yoga mat pushed into the corner of your room, folded rebounder mini trampette, a cookbook perfectly positioned for looks on your bookshelf that needs to stop smelling like it's just been printed - all these items in your home are living proof that you do think about your health, otherwise, why would you have spent your hard-earned cash on these and clutter your home?

A few years ago, at a seminar I attended, I learned that it's not about "shelf-development it's about self-development." If your mindset is still where it was, you cannot move forward. It's time to upgrade your thinking.

All kidding aside, exercises we can do on the lounge floor or in the park, combined with proper well-balanced nutrition, and you are on the way to enjoying vitality.

You just need to stick to those habits, and that's the challenge! We live in a day and age where we want things instantly; we look for magic pills and fast resolution.

However, would you agree that cheese or wine, a strawberry that has been given proper time and optimal conditions to mature, just taste so much better? Similarly, when we create the optimal environment for our bodies, the only thing it will lead us to is good health. Nature created an incredible apothecary. Have some faith and trust in nature and the produce it leaves on our doorsteps. When you have a choice, use raw, unprocessed, unrefined and naturally derived products.

Do not replace a healthy diet with supplements. Supplement, as the word suggests, means 'in addition to' not instead of. A 2014 study by Sheffield University indicated that our soils are continuously being depleted of nutrients; therefore, the produce available in the supermarket store is less nutrient dense than it was a decade ago. To satisfy our bodies need for nutrients, we need to eat more of the same type of food to get the benefit.

According to the latest 2021 statistics published by World Health Organisation, "9 billion adults are overweight or obese, while 462 million are underweight. Globally in 2020, 149 million children under 5 were estimated to be stunted (too short for age), 45 million were estimated to be wasted (too thin for height), and 38.9 million were overweight or obese.

Around 45% of deaths among children under 5 years of age are linked to undernutrition."

These statistics are alarming, especially as we learn that nowadays, the leading causes of death in the world are heart disease, cancer, diabetes, and respiratory diseases, most of which can be linked to our sedentary lifestyle. The Mintel 'Vitamins and Supplements' report dated September 2016 indicated that in the UK, 65% of adults had taken some form of vitamin or supplement daily or on an occasional basis in the previous 12 months.

If you are like me, you do your best to eat right, exercise, and take your nutrients. We all have days when we love to indulge, and that's OK, as long as you are in control of your sugar and not the other way round. Set and know your boundaries. You understand how important it is to take excellent care of your mind, body, soul. Stay as active as practicable and purchase natural supplements and functional foods rather than their poorly developed counterparts.

You are probably aware that adding good quality oil with vegetables helps your body better absorb nutrients. When exercising, think of combining cardio with moderate weightlifting as this can help you to stay fit.

Stretches and voluntary muscular specific movements help to unlock mobility in your joints.

Qi gong helps in multiple ways and calms your nervous system, but you may not know how to supplement to get the most out of your vitamins and minerals.

The truth is most of us swallow pills, not even thinking how they interact and whether they need another mineral, vitamin or food in order to interact and be absorbed within our bodies.

Here's some tips to get you started right away by implementing some simple habits.

- Stretch your body when you are just beginning to wake up; whether it's a baby pose or a full-body stretch, you can do it in your warm bed, and it does not take long.
- Start your day with room temperature glass of water with either lemon, infused garlic, or chlorophyllin to not only hydrate your body but remove toxic waste, as by 8 to 9 am, your bowel movements should be at their peak.
- Switch on that positive meditation or mindfulness podcast, open your curtains or blinds wide and greet the day, thankful for all good that comes into your life. Prime your mind and body.
- Use body brushing from time to time in the mornings; you will be surprised how much your circulatory system awakens and with it your energy levels.
- Build regular breaks for you in your day to unwind.

- Introduce movement into your day. The World Health Organization, Food and Agriculture Organization of the United Nations and the United Nations University reported in 2001 that the lack of exercise is undoubtedly related to civilization diseases and, above all, to the increase in the number of obese people in the world.
- To organise your thoughts and remove overwhelm, use journaling to get things off your mind and reduce anxiety.
- If you have invested in pure natural quality nutrients, pay attention to the small print about when and how to take them; they do come at a cost. There is a saying you get what you have paid for, so when I purchase them, I do everything I can to make sure my body absorbs them as much as it can.
- Sleep 7 hrs a day if you can, uninterrupted. Be aware of moon cycles, as studies of lunar cycles confirm that about five days before the full moon we sleep less than usual because the moon's gravitational pull increases, so your sleep tends to be disturbed. Leave your social devices on sleep mode and out of your room, at least an hour before bed.
- Eat for pleasure and to be content, not full, chewing your foods properly, slow down and eat mindfully, giving the body opportunity to digest and send signals back to you when you are becoming content

What are the no-no's when supplementing, and how is it best to take these nutrients?

- Do not take nutrients and vitamins at the same time as having coffee or tea, as both can act as an inhibitor. In fact, any food containing caffeine, chocolate, and sparkling beverages inhibits the benefits of vitamins and minerals. Properties in caffeine impede the uptake of nutrients and increase the rate at which they are excreted from the body. Sugar also has this effect. Do take with freshly pressed orange juice, as minerals are absorbed in the highest rates when paired with citrus fruit because of the high content of vitamin C or acidic foods.

- Have your natural supplements as part of your balanced meal. Fat-soluble vitamins such as Vitamin A, D, E, and K should be eaten with some fat. For example: at breakfast, make sure you add good quality fat; a bit of peanut or almond butter on your toast will do.

- If however you want to address and work on increasing your bone density or have muscular pains, you need to know that collagen supplements are best absorbed with vitamin C and D3, K2 MK7. Vitamin D works in symbiosis with calcium, and your body needs calcium to absorb vitamin D. However, excessive dietary calcium can impede the absorption of phosphorus or zinc, both of which are needed by our skeletal system. Magnesium is better absorbed with the presence of vitamin D, but calcium and magnesium in higher doses together can be problematic, as they both compete for bioavailability. I hope this example has demonstrated why the right synergy and each ingredient level of supplements are important to understand.

- Don't just pick up any supplement; choose one that you know will make a difference, and allow a minimum of 3 months for them to work - there is no magic pill. If you are deficient in certain nutrients, your body will give you visible signs, whether it is lethargy, struggling to fall asleep, or skin tone and nail condition. It's always worth checking for mineral and vitamin deficiencies with your GP. I ask to have a routine test to make sure I am not deficient. You allow finance and time for an MOT for your car; when have you allowed time and space for your body to have a full MOT?

- When taking amino acids, herbal supplements, or enzymes, researchers suggest that an empty stomach is a good thing. Most medical professionals agree that amino acids, enzymes, and herbs should be taken either 30 minutes before a meal or two hours after. By doing this, you are not risking any unnecessary interaction, and you may achieve optimal absorption.

- There is a fancy term these days for natural supplementation and the right nutrition that can help you feel more energetic and alert; you've probably heard it -

"biohacking." Researchers are looking at how nutrients affect our genetic makeup; these studies are called nutrigenetics. Fascinating if you are into this sort of thing. However, researchers also point out that nutrigenetics is not the complete answer to our vitality.

Our body is an amazing machine with fascinating abilities if we provide the right environment. Combine your habits to reduce stress, move, take time for yourself (no guilt attached), learn from nature, and stay as close as possible to non-processed foods. Do activities that require you to move, go outdoors and laugh a lot, connect with friends and families in a real, nonvirtual world whilst you still can.

The world is fast-changing, but it's up to you to decide what changes you accept and which ones you reject. Aristotle said, "We are what we repeatedly do; excellence then is not an act, but a habit."

What are your habits, and do they support your body, where you are or want to be? It is not all about epigenetics, deficiencies and our DNA; environmental factors and our habits also determine how we will feel in a few years or decades.

Refusing to participate and maintain good health seems to be secondary in today's humanity, even though we all know that you cannot buy health and supporting your body now will pay off later in your life. If we accept that our body is a connection of interdependent organs with specific needs, it's not a surprise that the answer to vitality is a multitude of positive behaviours and actions. Chris Argyris, Professor at Harvard Business School, summed it up for me "No one can develop anyone else apart from himself. The door to development is locked from outside".

If you have enjoyed this chapter and want to connect further, you can find me on social media, i.e. Facebook and Instagram or via my website. Healthy lifestyle changes and nutrition are my passion, and as a life coach, I may be able to help you upgrade your thinking and support you to make those lifestyle changes for incrementally and consistently.

Love your minerals, love your cells.

CHAPTER 2

Letting Go. The Art of Allowing

By Angela Maroosis

Language is a powerful force. Our ability to articulate ourselves to each other directly impacts how we experience connections. Words generate responses within us in emotional, mental, and spiritual ways. These responses are the catalysts for actions and inactions. It has been my personal experience to be triggered by certain words. To be triggered is to find myself feeling uncertain, vulnerable, and at times defensive. When I do not understand what is being asked of me, or I am afraid that what is being asked will be painful and represent the loss of something that I do not want to give up, I hold on tighter to try and alleviate the triggered feelings. Allowing triggered responses to remain a pattern in one's life is a vicious circle which leads to unhappiness, anxiety, and loneliness. The answer to breaking this pattern for myself came from being deeply curious and aware of what I wanted out of the confining darkness.

The term letting go was absolutely one of the most triggering to me because I believed I was facing another relationship or situation where I had to be the one to give up my dreams or desires. I was so tired of feeling lonely and left behind.

At times I felt victimized because other people's needs and wants were being met, and I was giving, but barely, if at all, receiving anything I would perceive as desirable. The answer to systematically altering my perspective and experiences started with the word *Agape*.

As a child, my Yaya, grandmother in Greek, would use this word to tell me that she loved me. She explained it as 'my heart and soul sees and loves your heart and soul.' Once I was old enough to understand, to me, it meant that we are beautiful and unique in our own ways. I felt like that is how it is meant to be. Agape is unconditional love, and while Yaya was offering it to me, she was also leading me to find it within myself for myself.

See, our triggers are very personal because they reside within us. They are the places where we do not feel loved. These are places we are meant to heal, for ourselves. The good news is that we are not alone in the healing. The connections that elicit triggers are also the places where we can manifest healing. I learned this by figuring out what letting go really means.

Letting go is actually a special kind of allowing.

This allowing involves giving ourselves permission to make space for our feelings, acknowledgements, and self-awareness. This process begins internally.

What you are doing is asking yourself who I am, what do I value about myself, and am I worthy of something more than I am currently experiencing?

The space you create within yourself by allowing, is for the purpose of potentials becoming their genuine expressions of who they really are. It also shows who each of us is in the connection. The space of allowing is a form of art because you are sculpting an experience with your ability to embrace and express agape. Agape is a place to build your dreams and heart's desires from.

Within the allowing you will need to assert yourself positively by first being clear about your feelings, words, actions, and intentions. As you discern for yourself the root of the trigger, you will begin to understand the belief that you hold that is limiting you and your potentials from becoming a reality. There is a natural cycle that exists within us and around us.

This cycle of energy asks us to be available to movement and change. Perhaps you have heard the term "go with the flow", this is not what most would believe it to be. You are not meant to permit your triggers to hold you hostage or to let other people and situations define who you are.

You have to do this for yourself. It is about recognising how you truly feel and working through the why, when, and how to make positive, healthy changes within yourself.

Here is where you learn to have and hold healthy boundaries, those appropriate yeses and no's that positively support who you know yourself to be. Healthy boundaries serve everyone in a connection because this is the place that fosters respect, honesty, and integrity. When you engage with another, these positive qualities combine in the true spirit of agape. Within this space you will need to trust your feelings and ask questions to both yourself and the other for the purpose of clarity. What are the underlying nuances between you and another? This is a conversation with yourself first to find your clarity and balance around your feelings and how to responsibly express them to another. You are 100% responsible for your feelings, words, actions, and intentions. So being clear with yourself is not only important, but necessary, in order to experience genuine healing and expression of what you value yourself worthy of.

When the conversation begins with the other person, you will need to be in the present moment and not allow their words to push you out of your internal clarity. Yes, they will have their own perspective, which may be in opposition to yours.

However, remember this is why you are having the conversation and did the internal process first. Let me be very clear that it is not your job to convince anyone of anything, nor should you be expected by another to be won over by their efforts of convincing you. As the dialogue between you unfolds, should you find yourself facing your need or another's to convince, I would ask you to step back graciously. The exchange of convincing is the dynamic of power and control, which does not positively serve either of you. Engaging in conversations, situations, or circumstances where one party's needs and demands must be met in order for a connection to continue is not healthy. Healthy connections are the only way to create healing and positive change in your life.

You do not have to attend every argument or discord you are invited to, but you do need to work through your feelings and find the healing you need and deserve. Spending your energy cultivating positive dialogues, compassion and understanding within yourself for who you are, is the way to embrace and experience positive life affirming changes.

Remember that you matter. Your feelings, words, actions, and inactions have real-world consequences for you. Take the time you need to discover and feel your way to the root of a trigger, and the reward is that you will experience agape.

Once you get a taste of self-love, you will strive and thrive at nurturing this within yourself and being available to the sincere reflection of it in the world around you. Negative or triggering situations are not meant to convince you that you failed or are not worthy of better, they arrive to be the catalyst of change.

The outcome of any change is determined by you because it is an experience that touches you deeply. What happens within you is under your control – the choice is yours. What do you desire to experience? How you attain your desired outcome is a reflection of who you are. Even if you choose to not engage in the connection, you are still receiving a positive and desirable outcome. This happens because you supported yourself with love, acceptance, and respect.

Where do you no longer want to invest your time, efforts, or resources? How do you want to feel when you get up in the morning and when you close your eyes at the end of your day? What is it you truly desire?

The shift comes from acknowledging that it is time to purge the old, those beliefs that make us feel stuck, the mindsets that keep us feeling confined and at the mercy of uncertainty in the world. Notice that these are all feelings. What is the origin of these feelings?

The answer is our beliefs. Beliefs can come from outside sources that tell us who we are or how we should feel, and then there are those beliefs we form internally. Interestingly the internal beliefs come from our direct experiences with the external world. Did you choose to accept someone else's outlook, or did you listen to another's belief and ask yourself whether you actually hold a similar feeling? Sometimes when we are looking for something to bring us a sense of peace, a desire for certainty that we can build and thrive upon, we muddy our own feelings by taking what someone else offers without actually thinking about our own experiences and knowledge.

The underlying nuance is a desire for positive change. Think of change as a butterfly. We cultivate change in our lives through the process of personal experiences and what we learn about ourselves. Everyone starts at the same point, birth, and we all meet the same ending, death, but what we experience between these points is our own personal transformation. Cultivating positive change is the experience of expanding the expressions of self-love.

The fundamental basis of self-love comes from understanding that we individually must define who we are, our values, our worthiness and what we believe love is. The beautiful thing about being human is that we possess feelings and an instinctual desire to thrive.

Feelings are very personal because they originate within us, and only we can directly sense them. Throughout our entire lifespan, we undergo numerous changes; however, the most profound seem to occur when we find ourselves triggered by external uncertainty.

How I strive to remain outside the black hole of feeling worried and fearful is by reminding myself that if I want better and know I deserve better, then I have to show up and do better.

Better means stretching yourself to do something different. Change is uncomfortable, but it is also innovative and necessary for you to expand and build the life you know yourself worthy of. The war within us is to hold healthy boundaries and allow ourselves to change.

Are you willing to look at your choices, actions, and patterns? Acknowledging and altering what you believe about yourself is the process of healing.

Who you used to be brought on the changes in your life thus far. Even if you feel worse, a part of you got better. A part of you just got by, a part of you survived, and a part of you thrived.

Whichever you relate to, the difference is you. You can make the changes when there is something to adjust to.

Taking on the challenges that life offers means breaking free from doubting who you really are. It is okay to feel lost, confused, or even invisible to the world. You have come a long way. You are Beautiful. You have sharpened. Can you see your courage, that beautiful strength within you that reaches out with faith, hope and trust that there is more to you than what other's see? Who is it that you see? What got better about you? What can you build on?

Who you used to be, is still here, but let's be clear, you got better, and you will continue to get better. Use that deep inner strength and courage that has brought you here to find all that untapped potential hidden deep inside of you, waiting to be used. Your potential knows no bounds. Your existence in the world makes a difference. Even if you do not yet know your worth. You are Priceless. You are One of a Kind.

The moment you have been waiting for, wanting, and hoping would arrive is right in front of you now.

Picture a large white canvas. This is a new chapter of life for you. Notice the crispness of the white. This white canvas is a clean slate, a place for you to build the vision of your dreams and heart's desires. As you gather your hopes, dreams, wishes and prayers together, allow yourself to feel the joy, happiness, and peace they express deeply within you.

Each one is a gift for you to experience and share out into the world in your own unique way.

Allow yourself time to bring clarity to each of these gifts. As you begin to feel more connection with your dreams and heart's desires, pick up the paintbrush and choose the colours that bring you joy when you express these to yourself. Do not hold yourself back.

This is your canvas, your life, and you are the artist. This canvas is the place of innocence within you, where your mind and heart align to support the beauty of who you are at your most sacred space, your soul. This is your dominion, a place where you are completely free beyond the confinements of physical time and space.

Take your time building this beautiful masterpiece, for as you feel the vibrancy of the energy, it will inspire you to create its essence in the world around you.

These sparks of inspiration are love being expressed to you. They are asking you to create them for yourself in your physical life. The effort is yours; however, you are not alone. You have a soul tribe.

These are the relationships and situations that are drawn to you with clear and positive intentions.

Your soul tribe shows up and offers hope, encouragement, and compassion in support of you being who you know yourself to be. There is no agenda, just unconditional love.

Place a beautiful gold frame around your masterpiece. This frame can have simple edges or be quite elaborate; the choice is yours. Why a gold frame? The element of gold represents mankind's heart, the incorruptibility of our natural design to strive towards thriving. Your life, like gold, is precious. You represent a star of pure light in the Universe, sacred for your own intrinsic value to the wholeness of existence. The frame is your healthy boundaries. These boundaries protect you on all levels of your being. They inform all those who step into your personal space that you know yourself, what you value, and your worthiness.

You will continue to grow, and your life will change. All of this is happening for you. It is natural because you have let go of the things you cannot control and allowed yourself to be the priority in your life that you were meant to be.

Words have the power to mask who you are, or to free you. Choose wisely what you say to yourself and others about who you are. Let no one steal your voice. Your personal power is to be the best version of who you are.

Allow yourself to speak your hopes and dreams, for these are the sparks of inspiration that are the gold within each of us.

Evolution requires change but do not fear that which may end because of change. Change is the gift that brings in something new to expand and grow your experience of a life fully lived.

You are worthy of happiness, as you are a gift and a blessing.

Life is a labyrinth of choices and consequences, each with surprising twists and turns that serve to remind you of your personal strength and power for good or ill. Here is the embodiment of the wisdom of timing in action and the courage to explore the unknown.

We are encouraged to develop a balance between independence and togetherness, harmonious relationships between light and dark, action and observation.

New opportunities to thrive are upon you now. There are no accidents or coincidences, as everything happens for a reason.

We all face uncertainty and make choices, but the key is showing up with the intention of honouring yourself wholeheartedly, including that which you may perceive as imperfections.

Here is where new hope begins that no matter what the journey ahead may bring, you will have happiness and gentler times. Enjoy your journey and remember that there are infinite potentials available, and your choices expressed with agape will support your new experiences. Let your heart and mind be filled with gratitude and love, for it will reveal the most amazing treasures within you that you could ever imagine.

The time has come to take a new approach to your life, which involves allowing yourself to experience more positive change.

You are doing a fantastic job of navigating your life. I know this because you are here reading this, and that is a sign that what is occurring within you is the emergence of your Authentic Self.

Letting go is the art of allowing yourself to cultivate positive changes within you that prepare and support you for investing yourself wholly in the authentic opportunities of nurturing, healing, and expanding your life. What you invest in yourself is what you have to invest in the world. Showing up and being an expression of love is a gift worth receiving and sharing.

CHAPTER 3

Loving Yourself from the Inside Out (Part 1)

By Angela Roth

A few years ago, I had the pleasure of visiting a well-hidden historical jewel in the Shropshire town of Craven Arms with my family. Twisting and turning, as we climbed the stairs, we were treated to visual insights into the last century at the fascinating 'Land Of Lost Content' museum. As our eyes took in the huge variety of everyday objects, regularly used in years gone by, the children were highly amused to see that toys and clothes we recognised from our own childhood were also on show, now displayed as historical artefacts!

Perhaps you're wondering where I'm going with this in a book about health, but you see, it made me realise how closely history follows us. Seeing at first hand the changes in clothes, toys, kitchen equipment and so on, I was fascinated that items I'd taken for granted in my childhood were simply improvements on those that had gone before.

There were very few totally new innovations displayed; even those that had seemed to be major new developments, like the first home computer, had an incredibly long history of research and development behind it.

Of course, historians have always been interested in understanding what took place in days gone by, but until relatively recently, they've had to rely on artefacts that have been unearthed, books, photographs, old parish records and so on piecing together stories passed down. Now, however, a whole new avenue is available in genetic research, showing how our genes describe our personal history – where our ancestors came from, the foods they ate regularly and more.

On a smaller scale, researching your Family Tree can also be deeply rewarding, but as I walked around that museum in Craven Arms, I began to wonder if there was another kind of history it would be invaluable to decipher.

You see, for over four decades, I'd lived as an emotional, or 'comfort' eater, something that had become part of my life after I was very badly bullied during my years at High School.

Chocolate had become my go-to comfort snack, along with other, generally, sweet 'treats'.

Trying a wide variety of diets, just like most others who are desperate to lose weight, I had spent many years yo-yo-ing up and down, sometimes feeling proud of myself, more frequently feeling ashamed. Having four children over twelve years had given me the excuse of using 'baby weight' to hide behind for longer than most of my contemporaries, but even that couldn't last forever.

Eventually, a family tragedy led me to re-examine my own weight problems and decide that I needed help, so I marched into the local weight-loss club, determined to get things sorted.

Armed with more willpower than I'd ever yet experienced, I read all the literature, bought all the recommended foods, and began to follow their plan. To my delight, the weight started to go, and I focused totally on making sure this continued, staying to group every week, and generally winning the 'Slimmer of the Week' award! As the weight fell away, I began to be scared that I would regain it just as fast – after all, that's what had always happened before, so I continued eating to lose weight beyond what was healthy, hitting the four stone mark after just four months.

By now, my sisters were telling me to stop; they were kindly pointing out that I was beginning to look older and rather unhealthy, but I didn't want to believe it.

I kept going to the group, hiding keys in the pocket of my heaviest jeans so that I wouldn't weight less than the lowest allowable weight for my height. What didn't register at all with me was that although I now wasn't eating the chocolate, biscuits, and cake, I was still an emotional eater - in other words, my eating habits were still controlled by my emotions, not by a desire to be healthy and consequently, I wasn't giving my body the nutrition it deserved.

The truth is, of course, that my actions were being strongly guided by how I saw myself on the outside; by how magazines and TV programmes suggested a woman should look if she wanted to be attractive. Without even realising it, I had believed all the media threw my way about how health should be determined; I just couldn't see it. Sadly, the weight-loss organisation didn't see it either – they didn't see that I wasn't living at a healthy weight, they didn't know what I was doing to my body, nor how I was convincing myself that I needed to lose more.

Eventually though, my weight sort of stabilised after I experienced a traumatic death in the family and some of my old eating habits returned. I had been horrified to see those all too familiar feelings of guilt and shame reappearing, and so I applied to be a consultant in the same weight-loss organisation

I'd lost weight with. Before long, I'd done the training and was running four groups of my own; I loved it! I felt as if I'd found my purpose at last, and I believed that standing at the front week in, week out, would give me the incentive I needed to keep my own weight under control. However, I couldn't have been more wrong.

As another major crisis landed in our family, this time the domestic abuse of one of our much-loved sons, my old eating habits launched themselves at me with a vengeance! The willpower I'd captured during my weight loss years escaped, disappearing without a trace. I was alone, supporting my lovely members as best I could, but knowing my heart wasn't in it at all, and feeling like a complete and utter fraud.

It was after several months, when my weight was threatening to reach its peak again, that our visit to the museum took place, and I understood that along with the history behind our Family Tree, every single one of us has a personal food story too. It's a story that goes way back before we were even born, a story that goes back down the generations and has coloured the way we eat and our behaviours around food today.

It's a totally fascinating story, one we need to explore, so we can finally understand our food choices; why some people live apparently free from any food battles while others have struggled for as long as they care to remember.

For the first time in my life, I began to look backwards, to discover when I had adopted behaviours around food that would cause me to spend my whole life feeling unhappy, guilty, and ashamed about my body.

Slowly, I began to realise that the bullies at school had left me so lonely that I had unintentionally sought the feeling of warmth and love we always shared as a family around our Sunday afternoon tea. You see, it was one of the highlights of my week; there were ten in our family, Mum, Dad, and eight children; we were happy, we were loved. Every Saturday, Mum would spend the day baking, smells of delicious cakes, scones and cookies emanating from the kitchen, the children taking turns to scrape the bowls! Sunday teatime would arrive, and the laden trolley was pushed into the lounge; it was the only day we didn't have to sit at the table; happy, lively chatter and laughter would abound, and I would be safe in that precious space, that warm space, that loving space. There, I could forget the bullies, their taunts and jibes; there I felt protected.

Recognising at last that I had adopted self-preservation tactics, recreating the family warmth and love, by buying chocolate each day after school, I began to feel a different kind of weight lifting from my shoulders; a weight that wasn't mine to carry any longer, and I chose to forgive those girls, who'd hurt me so badly. I chose to walk away from the pain and to let go of the shame and scorn they had poured into me.

I realised that they must have been carrying their own pain to treat me like that; but that ultimately, they had no right to control my self-belief (or lack of it); they had no right to take away my self-confidence, nor to steal the love for myself that I needed to live by – that we all need to live by. They had no right then, and they had no right now.

This was just the start of the journey I began to walk that day, but it was the beginning of the most powerful part of my story to date. It opened up a process I needed to take myself through – a process of self-discovery, self-acceptance, and self-love; but the most amazing thing of all, and the reason I'm telling you this story, is that it opened up a completely unexpected, unconscious desire within me to start loving my body in the way I had never been able to do up till that point. To feed it correctly, to nurture and cherish it, to care for it as the most precious gift I have ever been given – in other words, to love my body from the inside out.

CHAPTER 4

Loving Yourself from the Inside Out (Part 2)

By Angela Roth

As I stood there in the kitchen, the fridge door open before me, I could almost hear the chocolate bar I'd hidden weeks before calling out to me. That soft, subtle, velvety whisper, telling me that I'd feel so much better if I just took a quick bite or two while no one was looking; and it was so very tempting.

Have you ever been in that situation? Certainly, the chances are that if you've struggled with weight over the years, never feeling that you're the right shape or size for your height, feeling like a constant failure because you never seem to make it to the end of the diet and always trying to gather up enough willpower to start all over again; then you will recognise a scenario something along the lines of the one I've just described.

At times, of course, you will have turned away swiftly, shaking off the temptation easily, and continued with what you were about to do, such as eat the pre-chopped carrot you'd put in the fridge that morning for just such an occasion.

At other times, the inner battle you experienced will have been every bit as real as an argument the children might have had over who's turn it was on their favourite computer game – an argument you recognise as childish even, but nonetheless, just as real.

So where do these thoughts, these actions, come from? And how do you set about changing them? Unravelling the roots of any kind of emotional eating is at the very heart of the journey to freedom from them; indeed, as I discovered myself, it is at the very centre of the successful journey into living at your ideal healthy weight for good.

You see, as I referred to in my first chapter, each of us has our own unique 'food story'; this story began before we were even born – before our parents were even born in fact. It began as habits, customs, and opinions around food; how we eat, what we eat, when we eat and so on. Other people's decisions, opinions, and beliefs about food have played a part in shaping our lives from our very first sip of milk – or even colostrum - as a newborn baby, and they have carried on for many years past that day. Unlocking and deciphering them is the key to finding your way forward into the life you deserve, a life of living in the body you love.

The truth is that there is a very strong link between the taste receptors and the emotions - MRI scanners are now able to produce detailed maps of brain activity as prompted by different foods. They show that taste and smell are deeply interconnected with the brain's function and emotions. In one study, *Cornell food scientists discovered people in negative emotional states tend to crave sweets more than those in a positive frame of mind." This may come as no surprise to one who has struggled with emotional eating of course, but in this particular study, the subjects being investigated were players from college hockey games, not your most obvious emotional eater. The study examined how emotions arising from the outcome of each game influenced the perception of sweet, salty, bitter, sour, and savoury tastes. It was very noticeable that the players in the losing teams were much more likely to reach for the sweeter foods than those who had been victorious. The harder the defeat, the stronger the craving.

In most cases, not being able to clearly remember your early childhood is entirely normal; it's just the way the human brain works, with the average person being unable to remember specific events before the age of three.

This childhood amnesia isn't usually anything to worry about, but it's fascinating to note that even when the factual details remain forgotten, the emotional memories will often be invoked by tastes, sights, and smells.

Interestingly, whilst all three can act as precipitates, drawing out both positive and negative memories and feelings, leaving the subject emotionally moved in their aftermath, it seems that 'taste' memories can act the other way round. In other words, the emotion can first be experienced, followed by the need to source (or the craving for) the 'taste' memory of the food that the brain has creatively stored as a possible solution to the problem.

Anecdotal evidence also indicates that even when an adult's physical memory is impaired, by illness, for example, the emotions may still be relived through these senses, though more particularly those related to the sense of pleasure. My wonderful Father-in-Law, for example, has taken to eating a lot more chocolate as the vascular dementia he is sadly suffering from progresses.

It seems that the pleasure he takes from the taste comforts him, and this is certainly not unusual under such circumstances.

Of course, it should be noted here that the sense of taste and smell can both be impacted in more dangerous ways through such illnesses, leaving the sufferer confused about what is and isn't good for them to eat or drink.

This can lead to malnutrition, so care must always be taken to ensure a proper diet, but I can't help feeling glad that the 'taste' memory of pleasure lingers longest.

Furthermore, my own observations from working with clients across the world have led me to surmise that the link between the taste receptors and the emotions is even stronger than usual for emotional eaters. Our research so far isn't extensive enough to give a definitive answer, but I can confidently say that

I have seen a higher than average number of clients whose empathic personality directly correlates to the drive towards emotional eating. In other words, it would seem that those people who are generally of a sympathetic or compassionate nature may be more prone to emotional eating. Of course, I'm not saying that all compassionate people are emotional eaters, nor that all emotional eaters are empaths, but I have certainly seen a correlation and will continue in my own research to establish just how strong the link might be.

In the meantime, I will explain the thinking so far and explore how an emotional eater can choose to change that 'knee-jerk' response to eat when a 'taste' memory' is triggered.

An emotional connection can be described as a cluster of recollected feelings that come together to create a bond.

These feelings may be anger, sorrow, joy, love, frustration, excitement, or any of the myriad of emotions that humans experience. For most humans, food is frequently linked to powerful memories and emotions thanks to the 'information expressway' that connects chemical receptors in the nose, mouth and tongue, with parts of the brain devoted to emotions, thus creating that emotional bond.

While many chemical compounds are detected by the taste receptors, flavour is actually perceived as just one of six basic tastes: sweet, sour, salty, bitter, savoury, and fatty. Now, of course, any one of these can be attached to an emotional memory, and I imagine you will be able to recall one you associate with each of them, but for an emotional eater, the craving induced by a 'taste' memory will almost always be the result of a perceived need for positive reassurance of some kind. While this fact remains hidden or misunderstood, it is incredibly difficult for long-lasting change to be accomplished.

The emotional eater will battle long and hard to find the willpower to overcome the cravings but will never find the endless supply that would be needed - as 'any form of stress is the enemy of willpower'**, and who doesn't experience stress at one time or another?

So how can an emotional eater escape from the 'taste' memories that have made an emotional bond and seem to call them back when they least expect or want them to? Is it an impossible task, maybe something that should never be considered?

No, of course not! But such freedom will never be achieved by following suggestions such as, 'chop up a bowl of carrots to keep in the fridge'; or 'go for a run to keep you out of the kitchen'; or any of the other nonsensical suggestions I've heard propounded in my years working in the weight loss industry.

Neither will a successful outcome be obtained by substituting artificial sweeteners for sugar, fake 'oil' sprays for Olive Oil or highly flavoured, low-calorie snacks for wholesome, freshly prepared meals.

The answer lies in taking the pressure off, in giving yourself time to step back, allowing the opportunity to explore just where your 'taste' memories come from.

It's not an easy process; these memories will likely be attached to powerful childhood experiences, but most often, these are happy experiences, times when you felt loved, cherished, nurtured and/or protected.

They are not memories to be afraid of; they are yours to keep and savour, to store away and hold on to.

But in acknowledging them and recognising their power, you will be able to choose other, newer, less destructive ways to recreate the warmth and care your emotions are seeking to provide you with by drawing you to the 'taste' memories; and you will have taken the first steps to setting yourself free from the emotional eating that has been following behind you for far too long already.

CHAPTER 6

Connection: The Past and your Physical Body (Part 1)

By Aniko Hevizi

When it comes to physical health, our mental and emotional states play a big part. Many, if not all the time, the cause is subconscious, and we may not even be aware of it.

Before we dive in, there are two parts of the mind that are important to know more about if you are to understand why and how your body's health is functioning. The two parts are the conscious mind and the subconscious mind.

There's also a part that separates the two minds, which functions as a filter, called *critical faculty* (Dr Mike Mandel). This filter is only developed around the age of 6-7; before that, the subconscious mind is wide open and accepts everything presented to it without questions. What we heard, saw and experienced went right into the subconscious mind without filtering the untrue parts.

This is how other people's beliefs and habits have become ours. As we looked up to other people, we believed in their beliefs and habits and made them ours.

When children start to question what parents and authority figures are doing and saying to them, that's when the critical faculty is developing. Before that, they pretty much believe everything we say to them.

Your conscious mind is your logical mind. You are thinking and making decisions with it. You use your five senses, you see, you hear, you smell, you taste, and you touch with this part of your mind. The conscious mind has the ability to reject or accept any idea presented to it, and you can choose what thought you entertain and what you dismiss. Your conscious mind is aware at present, meaning it knows what date and time it is and where you are at the moment.

The subconscious mind is the emotional mind. This is the bigger part. All your memories and feelings are stored here, and your body and actions are controlled through your emotions. The subconscious mind is not aware at present, meaning past and future doesn't exist here. Only the now. This is why you are able to feel how you felt years ago if you bring up a memory.

Your subconscious mind remembers what emotions are attached to any memory, and it presents them for you with what you have in your mind.

The beauty of this is that when you go back in time and work on a past experience, releasing what doesn't serve you and heal what needs healing, the present and future will straight away change too. As the subconscious mind cannot differentiate past, present and future, it can only work in the now. Your timeline is in the present for your subconscious mind at any given moment.

This part of your mind doesn't have the ability to reject anything as it cannot think or be logical. It can only accept whatever is presented to it. Imagine it as Aladdin's Genie: "Your wish is my command!".

The subconscious mind has the most fascinating ability; it remembers everything, including the emotions that are attached to memories. And this is really good as long as we only have good memories filled with good emotions. But that's not always the case. We all have bad memories too, filled with unhelpful emotions that are painful and are holding us back.

What we usually do with these memories is bury them deep inside, so we don't have to keep remembering consciously and feel the emotions that are attached to them. If we did, we would be in distress a lot, if not constantly, from the emotional pain.

However, unfortunately, this doesn't work very well as those feelings are still there even if they are not showing themselves on the surface. They are 'alive' behind the scenes and doing what they know best, which is moving with all their pain.

This emotional mind controls your body too. Right now, while you are reading this book, you don't stop to make sure your heart is beating regularly or that your blood is flowing through your veins. All the physical functioning is done by your subconscious mind. It controls your body, including your actions, according to how you feel.

As emotion is energy in motion, it's constantly moving in your body and your energy field. It never rests, which is an important part you need to remember. Whatever you keep in your subconscious mind will express itself through your body. This expression happens either as a strong feeling, a behaviour, or when it's channelled inside the body it expresses itself as a physical issue in the case of a negative feeling (aches, pains, illnesses, dis-eases, stress, anxiety, panic attacks, and many other symptoms).

What I mean by channelled inside is a feeling that is pushed down and not acknowledged; then, as it has to move, it will move to a part of the body where it will express itself by making that part well or unwell.

These emotions and feelings are triggered by a thought that is either conscious or unconscious. Everything starts in your mind as a thought which generates a feeling that moves the body into action. Mind (subconscious) is movement, and the body is the manifestation of that movement.

When there's a problem in the body, that is a symptom of the mind (subconscious).

The word trauma usually makes people think of something really big and bad. What many don't know is that all events, situations, and experiences where a person doesn't have the right resources to overcome them can become traumatic.

If you didn't know how to talk about what happened, or you were not allowed to talk about it - perhaps there wasn't anyone around you who would understand and would be empathic to help you to overcome it - then you didn't have the right resources.

One of the right resources is a person at present who is understanding, empathic and wise enough to help us to overcome it. This means that we are given the opportunity to understand what is happening and are given some tools to find ways to let it go in a natural way.

Another is when we are allowed to talk about it to a person we trust and can receive some help to understand it and release it.

The right resource is also when we actually know how to overcome something. This means that we understand our own emotions, we know what they mean, and we have the ability to navigate them. Navigating our emotions means that we know what and how to release and strengthen.

In a situation, event or experience where we don't have the right resource to overcome it, we keep it, push it down and create a coping mechanism. This mechanism can become an issue later in life, but it can also cause trouble straight away.

What we keep and bury stays in our subconscious mind, in our energy field and body too. And as time goes on, and these emotions are trying to get our attention, they can become stronger and create issues in our physical body as well as in other parts of our life.

Beliefs play a huge part in our lives too. They can literally make or break things. We don't have to go far; just by thinking of politics, you know that what we believe in can divide a whole nation into two or more parts.

When we believe in something, we make sure that we live our life according to that belief. We choose our friends, our community and everything in our life in alignment with that belief. And this doesn't have to happen consciously, as it is deep-rooted, it navigates us unconsciously.

Our very first beliefs were created when we had no filter to question them in our first few years. These beliefs are often, if not always, other peoples' beliefs. As we had no ability to create our own, we borrowed other peoples' beliefs, and we made them ours.

Your parents', grandparents', and the people you looked up to or authority figures' beliefs became yours. And as the years went by, these beliefs were embedded so deeply into your subconscious mind that when you had the ability to question them, you didn't. Or at least not all of them.

When I say beliefs, I don't necessarily mean religious beliefs. I mean everything you believe about everything in life.

Including all that you believe about illnesses, about what happens in the body at a certain age, and about the mind and body connection.

For example, I have heard only horrible things about pregnancy and birth all my life. As these beliefs came from the people I looked up to, I believed them too. They became mine.

And so, my first pregnancy was really bad. My experience became traumatic, which ruined the beauty of it for me. My second pregnancy however was so much different. I worked on my beliefs, and as I released them, my experience changed, and I had a much better birth.

I would also like to mention here that everything you believe will happen to you because you hit a certain age, or because you do certain things, or because of your gender can be changed. In my personal opinion, if one person on this Earth can go through something differently, more beneficially, so can we.

What I would like to invite you to do is to check in with yourself. What do you believe about your age, about your physical state, about illnesses and dis-eases? Are those beliefs supporting you or perhaps holding you back? Are they really true? A simple yet such a powerful question to ask is, "Are these beliefs mine?".

They could be your parents', perhaps an authority figure's, or anybody else's. Make sure you filter them.

CHAPTER 6

Connection: The Past and your Physical Body (Part 2)

By Aniko Hevizi

When you are conceived, you already have your parents' DNA, genes and some of their beliefs, habits, emotions and traumas in yours. And your parents had their parents' DNA, genes and some of their beliefs, habits, emotions and traumas too when they conceived, and so on.

An important point here is to know that it's not your parents' or grandparents' fault what is happening in your life at all; this is how we all work as human beings. However, being aware of this information enables you to change whatever you want to change in your life. You can now make a connection between your physical health, your beliefs, your emotions and work on releasing and healing the wounded parts.

I invite you to look at things differently and start to work from the inside out. The majority of people work from the outside in, meaning they are trying to change their external world.

The people, the environment, the situations, even the weather, but that never works. Otherwise, we would all be happy and healthy at all times. The external world cannot ever be changed.

We can only change ourselves, how we feel at any given moment, which determines how we respond to things. And this response will generate a result. If we continue to blame the outside world for what's happening in our lives and react to it, we can never change anything. Start by changing your inner world, and your outer world will straighten too.

When things are not working the way you want them to, even though you are doing 'everything' right, you are most probably not touching the root cause. A physical pain or problem is a symptom of an emotional issue. And as I explained before, emotions are stored in our subconscious mind, which controls our body according to those emotions. If you want your body to change, to become healthier, you have to start with your emotions and feelings. And if you are not aware of them, remember they are buried. They need to be released so you can make space for the positive feelings to come to the surface.

When you are working from the inside out, you start by recognising the signs that are showing you that your emotional, mental or/and physical part needs attention.

I would like to share with you a list of common signs, although this list is not exhaustive.

- Unwanted behaviours like anger, drinking, overeating, etc.
- Reacting to things instead of responding in a calmer, more considerate way
- Negative, unhelpful habits
- Being too emotional too often and not being able to hold it together
- Weak immune system
- Aches and pains, especially chronic pain
- Illnesses
- Diseases
- Cold and flu regularly
- Negative thoughts more often than positive ones
- Unwanted outcomes
- Not being able to achieve goals
- Broken relationships more often than not
- Self-sabotage which is a huge one to remember
- Unnecessary worrying
- Anxiety, panic attacks
- Blocks
- Bumping into things
- Falling more often, yet there is no medical reason for it
- Dropping things

- Unnecessary stress
- Sleepless nights

Internal conflict is a sign too. When there is an internal conflict, we say, 'One part of me wants this, and the other part wants this'. Or we have a conversation in our mind about how we should have done that, or shouldn't have said that, to name just a couple.

And as those parts (emotions) are not in agreement, one is pushing you to do something, the other is pulling you away from it, and an energy state is created that you can imagine as a turmoil. Your body becomes weaker as this stress state is not healthy. Your mind, body and soul become unbalanced, and the positive or helpful feelings find it hard to show themselves.

When this happens, your body is in a stress state until the conflict is resolved. This can be turned inward, and your body suffers or can show itself through behaviours.

Other times you do something, and you don't know why you did it. That is when an emotion, or more than one, is buried from a past event and is trying to get your attention. It's hidden in a box, but as it is an emotion and it's moving, it wants to be acknowledged and healed.

It is trying to come out every now and then, but as it is really painful, the coping mechanism, which is a distraction, is switched on.

The distraction can be eating, smoking, or any other different kind of habit that is not so useful.

Whenever we lash out at someone for no apparent reason, we most probably have some emotions that need our attention too.

Again, one part of us is lashing out, and another will feel bad about it later on when the guilt hits us.

When it comes to mood states or parts, think about two or more people disagreeing. This is what is happening inside you too.

Two or more parts are in conflict and have no resources to come to an agreement because of their negative emotions and unhelpful beliefs that they are still holding onto from the past.

Once you have recognised that your mind and/or body needs attention, you move on to your thoughts and emotions to find out what is the cause. Meaning you find the connection between thoughts, emotions and physical body. Then you start working on them by shifting them.

You check in with the beliefs and emotions you are holding onto and are negative and unhelpful so that your body can become free and start to heal itself.

As you are changing your inner world, your outer world is also changing.

Your body becomes emotionally lighter (it can also become physically lighter), and as a result, it becomes healthier.

It also starts to function in a way that is supporting you. Aches and pains can be reduced, illnesses and dis-eases visit you less and less, and your immune system becomes stronger and healthier. Even your sleep will get better too.

The unwanted negative emotions will shift, and the more positive ones will become stronger and stay with you for longer, especially if you maintain the new state. Anxiety, panic, worry and stress will turn into calmness and self-assurance, reaction becomes response, and old habits will support you rather than being against you.

As you start to feel better and better within yourself, about yourself and the world around you, negative thinking will start to shift to positive, and that will charge up those good feelings even more.

As things are changing in your life for the better, your relationships will improve (I believe there's always room for improvement), and your outcomes will be the ones you actually long for. You will be able to achieve your goals much more easily and follow your true desire.

Overall, letting go of negative emotions, healing traumas and changing limiting beliefs allows your mind, body and soul to be in alignment and balance, and it allows you to live your life to the fullest.

I want to take the opportunity to say never dismiss medical advice. All the information I am giving you is extra, and it doesn't replace medical help.

CHAPTER 7

Be Kind to your Cholesterol

By Anita Andor

CHOLESTEROL 101

"Your cholesterol levels are way too high" – I am guessing you may have heard this from your doctor over your lifetime. While high cholesterol levels mostly enjoy a lousy reputation, I am here to tell you that there is no such thing as bad or good cholesterol. You will appreciate my thinking by the end of this chapter!

Some of the upcoming paragraphs may feel slightly dry, but it is vital to widen our knowledge base and debunk some cholesterol myths. You will recognise some of the upcoming players from your regular blood test.

What exactly is cholesterol?

Cholesterol is a sterol, a combination of steroids and alcohol molecules that dissolves easily in fat. The human blood is mainly composed of water, so any molecules soluble in water can travel on their own.

Molecules that dissolve in fat, such as cholesterol, and fat-soluble vitamins such as A, D, E, and K need a carrier to safely reach their destination. Cholesterol is transported in lipoproteins and other substances such as triglycerides, phospholipids, proteins, vitamins, and antioxidants. Lipoproteins are like a taxi service.

Lipoproteins are classified based on their fat and protein density. Hence the name, high-density lipoprotein (HDL) or low-density lipoprotein (LDL). However, there are more players in the game, and I would be lying if I said lipid metabolism is easy to understand. Let's give this a go, shall we?

The primary sources of triglycerides and cholesterol are from the diet or are produced by the liver. We must make a distinction between the functions:
- Triglycerides store unused calories for later
- Cholesterol builds cells and hormones

Dietary lipids are packaged into chylomicrons in the intestines. Chylomicrons are mainly composed of triglycerides with a minimal amount of cholesterol. They transport triglycerides from the intestines to muscle and fat cells and cholesterol to the liver.

Meanwhile, the liver is making very-low-density lipoproteins (V-LDL) which transport triglycerides and cholesterol to the body from the liver. Therefore, both chylomicrons and V-LDL are triglyceride-rich. The liver produces low-density lipoproteins (LDL) from V-LDL via a complex process. Then the last step is to make high-density lipoproteins (HDL) in the liver and the intestines. HDL picks up the remaining triglycerides, cholesterol, and other beneficial substances from the body and transports them back to the liver. Therefore, LDL and HDL are much richer in cholesterol than triglycerides.

Are you confused yet? I don't blame you, lipid metabolism and understanding cholesterol markers were one of the most complex processes I learnt in school, and there is more to come! I hope that the "Tunnel Analogy" will equip you with even more knowledge and you will be singing "I can see clearly now".

Players in The Tunnel Analogy:
1. lipoproteins as cars or taxis that carry around cholesterol and other fatty substances in the blood
2. cholesterol as passengers of the car
3. blood as the road the taxis driving on
4. blood wall as the wall of a tunnel

Any driver knows that the more cars are on the road, the more likely a crash will occur.

The collision of the cars damages the wall of the tunnel. This is precisely what happens to the thin and delicate blood vessel walls. Damage to the blood vessels calls for plaque formation, but more on that later.

It is evident that the number of cars (lipoproteins) creates a risky situation, not the passengers (cholesterol).

LDL or HDL cholesterol markers only tell us about the passengers, but we need to know the number of cars on the road, the driving factor of cardiovascular risk. Testing for such information is not part of a routine cholesterol panel. Nutritional and other integrative practitioners always request such markers as part of their screening process. LDL particle number (LDL-P) is one of them. LDL-P represents the number of cars on the "road' in our analogy. Looking into the size of the LDL particle is also a great addition to the panel, as these lipoproteins present with different sizes. The smaller the particle, the more likely it will penetrate the blood vessel wall.

Having said that, these are just markers. That does not mean cardiovascular disease is written on our forehead. It just means that there is a higher risk of having cardiovascular issues.

LDL particles have a limit as to how much they can carry.

For example: if the triglycerides are too high, they carry less cholesterol. The liver produces more LDL particles to carry that cholesterol left out in response to this. The result is an increase in the number of LDL particles. Therefore, doctors may refer to LDL as bad cholesterol because if LDL particles are high, it is likely that LDL will be high too.

You may be thinking, what causes elevated LDL-P?

- High triglycerides
- Thyroid issues: thyroid hormones influence lipid production, absorption, and metabolism and slow down the clearance of LDL.
- Infections such as Chlamydia pneumoniae and H. pylori as cholesterol levels increase to fight the infection.
- Leaky gut: LDL has anti-microbial properties and aims to clean toxins produced by gut bacteria leaking into the blood.
- Genetics: Elevated cholesterol might be due to mutations of specific genes. If you fancy checking them out, look at APOB, LDLR, LDLRAP1, and PCSK9.

But hold on, what is the big fuss and debate about the importance and the role of cholesterol? First, let's look at the main functions.

1. Component of the cell membrane

Every human cell is protected by a cell membrane separating the inside from the outside environment. The cell membrane decides what enters and leaves the cells. The integrity and the strength of the cell membrane are fundamental for proper biochemical processes to occur. Cholesterol modulates the fluidity and the permeability of the cell membrane.

2. Precursor to steroid hormones

With the help of cholesterol, we make pregnenolone which is the precursor to other steroid hormones. Pregnenolone is then further converted into progesterone. Next, progesterone is converted into androgens, and finally, androgens are converted into oestrogen. Insufficient cholesterol levels bring about hormonal deficiency.

3. Bile Acid Production

Bile acid is produced from cholesterol in the liver. Bile acid is essential for fat digestion, glucose metabolism and acts as an emulsifier for fat. New studies confirm that it is also a signalling molecule. It is stored in the gallbladder.

4.   Vitamin D production

The presence of cholesterol in the skin is a prerequisite to producing Vitamin D from exposure to sunlight.

5.   Fat-soluble vitamin absorption

As the name suggests, some vitamins can only be absorbed in fat. They must be emulsified and packaged into micelles that contain cholesterol.

6.   Nerve Cell Function

Cholesterol is needed to form the myelin sheath, a fatty substance wrapped around the nerve cells. The myelin sheath insulates as well as encourages electrical signalling. Recent studies are now investigating the beneficial role of cholesterol in conditions such as Multiple Sclerosis and Alzheimer's.

Eliminating cholesterol is as important as producing it. Cholesterol leaves the body via bile which brings me onto cholesterol gallstones...

Gallbladder motility (contraction and relaxation) is responsible for the optimal flow of the bile into the digestive tract. If the motility is compromised, cholesterol gallstones can be formed.

Why is this an issue since we said cholesterol is good? Well, cholesterol crystallises if it remains in the bile for too long.

An over enthusiastic liver that produces too much cholesterol married with a sluggish gallbladder may be a recipe for disaster.

Oral contraceptives, pregnancy, anti-cholesterol medications, rapid weight loss, obesity, excess fat intake, and Crohn's disease contribute to cholesterol production in the liver. Cholesterol can crystallise in the blood vessels too.

Statins

Cholesterol is made in the liver from a molecule (acetyl-CoA) involved in glucose, protein, and fatty acid metabolism with the help of an enzyme, HMG - CoA reductase. Enzymes help us metabolise molecules by either building or breaking down substances. Medicine usually is "programmed" to either block or stimulate the work of an enzyme to decrease or increase biochemical reactions. Statins inhibit the enzyme HMG - CoA reductase. Sadly, statins are the most commonly prescribed drugs globally and most probably very much over-prescribed. It seems the "normal" range for cholesterol got tighter and tighter over the years.

It should be noted that there are very unpleasant side effects of statin, namely:

- Sexual dysfunction
- Type 2 Diabetes
- Hormonal Dysfunction
- Neurological issues
- Muscle related issues

Another common issue is the depletion of CoQ10, an antioxidant naturally produced by the body. It is needed for energy production, cardiovascular health, and glucose metabolism. Therefore, complimenting statins with a CoQ10 supplement is highly recommended.

INFLAMMATION AND CARDIOVASCULAR HEALTH

To understand cardiovascular disease or any other modern disease for that matter, we need to deep dive into inflammation. Talking about inflammation, without a doubt, is one of my favourite topics. Reducing inflammation is the answer to way too many health concerns.

Inflammation is an immune system response, a natural defence mechanism to protect and heal the injured and damaged areas.

While acute inflammation is an essential and safe response, chronic inflammation will eventually cause diseases such as arthritis, inflammatory bowel disorders, allergies, asthma, and cardiovascular problems.

The most important question: What causes inflammation?

- Infections caused by viruses, bacteria and parasites by way of releasing toxins
- Excessive immune reactions such as food sensitivities and allergies
- Chemicals and irritants
- Lack of oxygen due to inadequate blood flow
- Sugar promotes free fatty acid production in the liver triggering inflammation. In addition, sugar wraps around protein structures, causing irreversible damage. For that reason, it needs to leave the blood quickly. That is why good insulin sensitivity is so important, as, without insulin, sugar can't get into the cells.
- Smoking and alcohol

Inflammation plays a significant role in every stage of plaque formation. As I mentioned earlier, the blood vessel wall is very delicate. Each time there is an injury to the blood vessel's division, the body sends an army of immune cells to fix the damaged area.

As a result, the wound looks like a microscopic scratch. If this happens over and over again, scar tissue forms. The vicious cycle leads to narrowing of the blood vessels and obstruction of blood flow to the heart (coronary heart disease), the brain (stroke), and other parts of the body, causing very sluggish circulation.

Cholesterol and lipoproteins are not to blame for cardiovascular issues. They are peacefully travelling in the blood; however, they clamp together and cannot pass through the damaged site due to the narrowing of the blood vessels.

Other gangsters are regularly joining the plaque formation party! As a result, toxins from plaque formation are consistently expelled into the coronary circulation. This is very important as it is the most critical blood supply in the human body.

The gangsters are immune cells, calcium, inflammatory cytokines, and oxidised LDL. The plaque starts off as a soft bulb then hardens due to calcification. According to BHF(British Heart Foundation), calcification occurs because the muscle cells change into bone-like cells in the blood vessel wall due to ageing. However, calcification is not the only "hardening" factor; cholesterol can also crystalise. This is seen both in atherosclerosis and cholesterol gallstones. Other risks on the list are ulceration and thrombosis.

Inflammatory Markers

The most common markers we use are C-reactive protein (CRP), erythrocyte sedimentation rate (ESR), and white blood cell count. Elevated ferritin levels are also taken into account. CRP is an early indicator of acute inflammation. It is more sensitive and specific than ESR.

Not an exhaustive list, but high blood pressure, smoking, cancer, diabetes, metabolic syndrome, exercise, burns, injury, or acute bacterial or viral infections can all cause elevation in CRP.

On the other hand, ESR gives us a better understanding of whether inflammation is chronic or not. It takes more time for ESR to "react", while CRP will be elevated and peak in the first 48 hours of a disease process.

Once the acute inflammation is resolved, CRP returns to the normal range within 7 days. It is best to order both if someone presents with chronic issues.

HORMONES

I am still amazed at how clever and complex the human body is. Hormones are so powerful, and they should be more respected and appreciated by our actions and choices.

Hormones are the chemical messengers in the body giving instructions for the cells on what to do.

Poor food choices, sedentary lifestyle, and genetics are not the only risk factors for cardiovascular disease. In addition, hormones such as insulin, adrenaline, cortisol, testosterone, and thyroid affect endothelial function.

Insulin and glucose are famous for their, well, occasionally troubled marriage. Without insulin, the blood vessels would be chronically flooded with glucose. With each meal consumed, blood glucose level rises. The pancreas releases insulin so that muscle and other body cells can uptake the glucose from the blood. The problem is that when blood glucose rises too rapidly, the pancreas releases too much insulin, which makes us feel tired again. We call this the blood sugar rollercoaster. Many foods cause blood glucose spikes, and most of us are aware of them but lack the willpower to make healthy lifestyle changes.

Glucose and insulin work together by a negative feedback mechanism. When blood glucose rises, the receptors on the cells sense the change. The pancreas is alerted to release insulin until a balance is achieved.

Glucose is a very sticky substance, it wraps around protein, causing irreversible damage, so it needs to leave the blood as soon as it serves its purpose. Any excess glucose is stored in the liver and fat tissue. If there is constant consumption of sugary foods - and no, we are not talking about chocolate only – the pancreas is constantly releasing that insulin.

There are two issues here:
1. The pancreas gets tired and eventually won't be able to produce insulin
2. The receptors on the cells become unresponsive in utilising insulin.

Consequently, blood glucose and insulin remain elevated as the process isn't working. We call this insulin resistance, leading to health concerns such as Type 2 Diabetes and Polycystic Ovarian Syndrome.

Following on from insulin, stress-related hormonal imbalance and weight gain, particularly belly fat, are the most significant health challenges my clients want to resolve.

Stress is a highly used word but do we really understand what cortisol is for and how it affects our health?

It is very common to experience the following while someone is highly stressed:

- Increased appetite and food cravings
- Increased body fat, especially abdominal fat
- Increased anxiety
- Decreased muscle mass
- Decreased libido
- Decreased immune response

Cortisol ensures that we have sufficient glucose in the bloodstream to fight. Through a feedback mechanism, glucose, fatty and amino acids are released into the blood for energy production. Drawing amino acids from the skeletal muscle to the blood continuously leads to the loss of muscle mass. Muscle is metabolically active; this means it burns calories at rest too. It is apparent that without muscle mass and movement, the body piles upon weight.

But why are we prone to deposit fat around the middle? The answer is prolonged and elevated cortisol levels. Cortisol influences fat distribution and favours depositing fat close to the liver, where it can quickly convert back to energy when needed. Remember that extra sugar and fat are stored in the liver.

Meet the HSD enzyme and testosterone

HSD enzyme

Fat cells contain an enzyme called 11 beta-hydroxysteroid dehydrogenase. Let's stick to HSD, shall we? The function of this enzyme is to convert inactive cortisol (cortisone) to active cortisol, which signals the fat cells to store fat mainly in the belly region. HSD activity tends to increase with age.

Testosterone

Elevated cortisol suppresses testosterone levels responsible for lean muscle mass and stamina. Low testosterone is presenting as fatigue and an increase in body fat. Loss in muscle tissue results in a reduced basal metabolic rate which affects calorie-burning capacity.

Belly fat is different from other body fat because it is metabolically active. In addition, it produces hormones and inflammatory agents.

Decreasing HSD enzyme activity and increasing testosterone levels are crucial in reducing belly fat.

To reduce HSD activity

- Consume foods rich in flavonoids such as apple and onion (quercetin), grapefruit (naringenin), and the most powerful one is orange. Please note grapefruit can interact with many medications.

- Non-GMO organic soybeans contain daidzein and genistein.
- Liquorice contains glycyrrhetinic acid (not to be used in the long-term due to its blood pressure complications), a type of flavonoid. It is also a great adaptogen, anti-inflammatory, protects the gut lining, and supports detoxification.

To increase testosterone

- Zinc is needed for testosterone production; however, please note it must be balanced with copper.
- Cordyceps mushroom powder also improves stamina and energy.

MY TOP TIPS TO SUPPORT HEALTHY CHOLESTEROL LEVELS

- Use only unrefined cold-pressed oil. Olive oil is highly recommended, but flaxseed, evening primrose, and black currant seed oils are also welcome.
- Replace wheat and white rice with oat bran and brown rice.
- Drink freshly squeezed carrots, celery, and beet juice.

- Avoid fried, burnt, and fatty foods and reduce meat intake.
- Mind your sugar intake to keep inflammation in check.
- Increase garlic and cinnamon consumption.
- Consider supplementing with a good liver support complex, chromium picolinate, Coenzyme Q10, and vitamin C.

Sadly, orthodox medicine only suppresses numbers and symptoms without investigating what is causing specific health concerns. Plastering a symptom only provides temporary relief and gives you false hope that everything works as it should.

I hope you found valuable information in this chapter and gained a better understanding of the importance of cholesterol and how it affects hormonal and cardiovascular health. My main goal was to stroke your interest in improving your overall health.

The human body is like a tree, so getting to the root causes of symptoms is your passport to longevity. Accomplishing physical health cannot happen without understanding human physiology.

CHAPTER 8

A Story of Two Bobs (Part 1)

By Dean Palfreyman

Introduction

This is a comparative story of two Bobs; they both have the same genetics and physiology however they live in very different times. Bob A lived approximately 250,000 years ago at the dawn of modern man; millions of years of evolution and natural selection have allowed his species, homo-sapiens, to thrive living alongside the other millions of species that populated the planet. Bob B lives in the 2020s; born into the modern world, he lives a very different life.

Both Bobs, as all life on earth, have one thing in common to live long enough to pass down their genes to future generations, and ideally to do this while living a healthy and happy life. Both of their potential lifespans would have been the same, however Bob A would be more likely to have died from injury, infection or starvation at an earlier age. Bob B may have medical interventions and sufficient food lending itself to a longer life, but is it in good health?

For the majority of human existence, we have lived as hunter-gatherers, then approximately 10,000 – 12,000 years ago, life began to change, we started to grow crops and become more settled in one place, the agricultural revolution had begun, slowly moving us away from our nomadic hunter-gatherer lifestyles to that of farming and villages and ultimately the modern world. This transition has allowed us to become the dominant species on the planet, feeding the millions but to what detriment? This is where our story begins.

Good Morning Bob A

The warm glow of the sun rising slowly over the horizon touched Bob's face, gently waking him from his rejuvenating sleep. He opened his eyes, took a deep breath, stretched and looked around. His two younger brothers were climbing a nearby tree, other members of his small tribe were rising from their slumber, and two elders were discussing the best direction to move next.

Bob was thirsty; he got up and walked slowly over to the stream that wasn't far away. He squatted down and cupped his hands in the water, bringing them to his mouth, he took a long sip then went back for more. He splashed his face, refreshed, he stood and looked into the distance, simultaneously contemplating the weather, the sounds around him and monitoring for any potential dangers.

He slowly began to head back to the camp; on the way, he passed three members of his tribe heading down to the stream carrying conical shells they used as water holders on long trips.

As he approached the camp, everyone was now awake and preparing to get ready for the day. A day Bob hoped would bring them more luck than the previous two, the hunt had not gone well.

The path was set, the elders started to lead the way, picking up the few possessions they had, basic tools, weapons and a few reserves of nuts found close by; they were on the way.

Good Morning Bob B

Blah, Blah, Blah, the shrieking noise of the alarm clock shocked Bob into consciousness; he quickly hit the snooze button. Ten minutes later, the same noise, "surely it's not time already", Bob says to himself, "I need more sleep". After lying there for a few more minutes, Bob drags himself out of his bed; his body aches, he stretches, yawns and walks to the bathroom. He looks at himself in the mirror, dark shadows under his eyes and looking exhausted, he washes his face. Feeling a little better, he heads to the kitchen and makes a coffee to give himself a boost.

As he sips his coffee, he reads the daily misery and scrolls through reams of social media on his phone; through the wall he hears his neighbours shouting at the kids to get dressed for school or they'll be late. Late! What's the time? He runs upstairs and has to catch his breath at the top; as he hurriedly dresses, he realises just how hungry he feels, tummy grumbling and a bit light-headed; he heads back to the kitchen. He quickly makes a bowl of frosted cereal and puts a pop-tart in the toaster to have in the car.

Grabbing his phone, wallet and keys, he rushes out the door, gets into his car; he's on the way.

Have a good day Bob A

The elders signal that they were headed towards the valley, a path that would lead them through an open glade and into a small wooded area where they hoped the gatherers would find some food. As they walked, Bob breathed deeply, took note of the sun on his skin; he felt good and hoped today would be fruitful.

The walk was going at a reasonable speed, some of the youngsters were slowing down, so their mothers picked them up to keep the pace.

They were approaching the tree line; this is where the females and children of the tribe would temporarily leave the older males to forage in the undergrowth for edible nuts, seeds and fungus.

Hopefully, they would dig up some tubers and maybe even find some fruit if they were lucky. Bob watched them branch off; they moved without thought as the environment dictated, crouching low, squatting, stretching high, stepping over awkward branches that got in the way. Bob would normally be with them, but not today as today was his first hunt.

He followed on with the elder males, the terrain started to become rocky, and he had to be more aware of his step, balancing and occasionally jumping from boulder to boulder. Up ahead, the leaders were crouched down looking at the ground. Bob caught up; they had found tracks; the hunt was on.

Have a good day Bob B

The next set of traffic lights turns red just before Bob gets to them, frustrated he takes a bite of his pop-tart; his stress levels are high even before starting work. He notices a twinge in his back, "hopefully it won't stop me getting to the gym later", he says to himself, feeling the ever-increasing roll of fat on his stomach. He can't understand why he's putting on weight, eating everything in moderation and trying to exercise.

Eventually, he gets into work, presses the button on the lift, he could take the three flights of stairs, but he's still tired. He gets to his desk just in time, slouches into his chair and logs onto his computer. Half an hour later, he gets up to go to the coffee machine; as the coffee pours, he can't take his eyes off the vending machine next to him; back at his desk, he opens the chocolate bar.

His morning goes slowly, but lunchtime comes around; he gets up out of his chair a little light-headed and tries to stretch out his back which seems to be getting worse. "You coming to the Café for lunch?" asks one of his colleagues. "Yes," he replied, disappointed that once again he had forgotten to bring a healthy lunch with him.

The afternoon goes a little better; a colleague had a birthday so a slice of cake helped.

Get moving Bob A

The Hunters move low and slow through the undergrowth, they are on the trail of a wild boar. Bob is on high alert, holding his spear tightly, waiting for the sign to pounce. A signal to stay still is given; they all squat down quietly, there is movement up ahead. After what seems like an age, he hears one of his tribe jump up and launch his spear, it hits, but it is not a clean shot.

The boar takes flight, and the hunters quickly follow, sprinting, jumping their way through the bush. Another spear flies, this time hitting its mark, and the boar drops to the ground; they all rush in spears drawn just in case, these creatures can be dangerous, especially if injured. Catching his breath, Bob sees that it is dead; he has a deep respect for the creature but is pleased that his tribe will eat well today.

The elders show Bob how to lash the boar to a branch for transport; they tell him that it is his and another younger member's responsibility to bring it back to camp. They both take an end of the branch and lift it to their shoulders; it's heavy, so it's slow going, but they both get back to their new camp where they are greeted by the women and children who also had a successful day's forage.

Get moving Bob B

Bob logs off his computer; he has hardly moved all day but feels exhausted. He looks at his phone; there is a message from his friend, "still coming to the gym?" it reads. Sighing, Bob replies, "meet you there", he really can't be bothered but knows he should.

In the changing room he checks his phone, another message, "I'm running late, get started without me". Bob steps up onto a treadmill; he hates exercise but knows it is good for him.

He sets the Fat Burn programme and begins to walk; as he does, he looks around at the shiny machines wondering what to do next. The treadmill starts to speed up; Bob presses the down arrow to override it, he doesn't want to overdo it.

After 10 minutes he checks his phone again, his friend wasn't going to make it. That's the only excuse Bob needs, he'll go and have a sauna instead.

What's for dinner? And good night, Bob A

Bob's small tribe sit around the fire; pieces of now butchered boar are laid across rocks to cook. Bob was looking forward to the food, he hadn't eaten more than a few nuts and a couple of berries since yesterday. The meat is handed around equally, and the tribe feast, Bob was lucky enough to receive some liver as a reward for taking part in his first hunt. They also had some tubers and mushrooms found by the gatherers.

After eating, the tribe sit close to the fire for warmth and safety; as Bob stares at the flames, his eyes begin to close, and he drifts off to sleep.

What's for dinner? And good night, Bob B

Bob returns home from the gym; he enjoyed his sauna but feels light-headed and starving; he realises he hasn't eaten for 3 hours!

He opens the fridge; there's some wilted salad that hadn't been opened and some margarine. Not much of a meal, he had forgotten to place his online food order.

He picks up the phone and speaks to his friendly takeaway owner. His dinner arrives in good time, and Bob slops it out of the plastic container onto his plate. Sitting in front of the television, he wolfs it down. Feeling stuffed and bloated, Bob takes his plate to the kitchen and grabs a coke from the fridge.

He sits back down in front of the television, where he stays until late, and he realises how tired he is.

Lying in bed, he checks his phone again to see if his latest social media post has any likes; he scrolls through the feed and eventually tries to settle down. As he tosses and turns, he wonders why he just can't sleep, he's exhausted.

CHAPTER 9

A Story of Two Bobs (Part 2)

By Dean Palfreyman

Lessons to learn from Bob

I'm sure as you read through the two Bob's stories, you will resonate more closely with Bob B as we live in the modern world. Although we will never have a day totally like Bob A in this time, what lessons can we take from it?

Hopefully, as you read their stories, you can see the stark differences between how we live in our modern world compared to our ancestors. So how can we use these comparisons to help better our health? There are many factors to consider, but I'm going to break things down into four principles, Sleep, Environment, Movement and Food; all four have cross overs and should become a foundation to help improve your health.

Good morning

How do you feel in the morning? Do you struggle like Bob B to get up?

Although I'm not expecting you to sleep outside, our ancestor's circadian rhythm would have been much more in sync with nature.

We would sleep as the sun set or soon after and wake with the sunrise. Our sleep would be more restful without the influence of caffeine, sugar, alcohol, EMF's, and bright lights throughout the day. Sleep is fundamental to our health; it's a time for rest and repair, to reset and prepare us for the following day.

After sleep, you should feel rested and ready for the day, not having to be startled into wakefulness, not needing a caffeine hit just to get you started. If your metabolism is working well (using stored fat), you shouldn't have to be reaching for the sugary breakfasts to fuel the first part of your day; this initial energy boost will run out quickly, leading you to crave more.

So what can you do to help?

Try and get into a routine of when you go to bed and wake up each day; this helps set your circadian rhythm helping you fall into a much more restful sleep.

Don't drink caffeine after midday, caffeine is a stimulant it can give you a quick pick up throughout the day, but it can also keep you awake at night.

Turn off all screens for as long as possible before bedtime; they emit blue light (just like the sun) telling your brain it's daytime; the same is true for home lighting keep them on a low dim or just have a single lamp.

Keep your bedroom cool and remove all electronic devices; they give off EMF's that can disrupt your sleep cycles.

Have a good day Bob

Both Bobs are trying to do the same thing each day - attain food - one via hunting the other by making money to buy it.

Bob A's food won't come to him, he has to find it in his environment. To do this he must move, walking lots, sprinting, squatting, lunging, lifting, throwing and jumping. Mixed with periods of relaxation and rest in the fresh air and sunshine.

Bob B has food available at all times and doesn't need to go far to find it. Snacks in vending machines at work mean he only needs to get out of his seat and walk a few meters for his next sugar fix. He spends most of his day in one spot, seated in one position, with artificial lighting and air conditioning, only having at most an hour to eat again and try and get his mind off work.

I appreciate you have to work however a few simple changes can improve your health and productivity.

Try and move more regularly throughout the day, set an alarm to remind you to get up, move or just change position. Small movements all add up, helping you stay mobile and reducing chronic stress. Stand up while taking phone calls or walk while you talk. Make the most of your breaks, ideally get outside for some fresh air and sun.

Get moving Bob

In Bob A's world, he is always on the move, exercising is not a thing, it's just a way of life. Our in-built survival mechanism saves energy; to actively try and burn more is unnatural, so it's not surprising that it's hard for Bob B to get motivated to exercise.

The type of movement is also very different; in the modern world many people outsource their lack of activity with the gym, long cardio sessions and perhaps some weight training. This is better than nothing, but the movements are generally not how the body should move and can lead to injury.

Finding some kind of exercise you enjoy is really important, but do try and keep things varied and target the whole body in multiple planes of movement. A mix of cardio and full-body resistance exercise is great but don't neglect your mobility.

Try to exercise outdoors; there are many benefits physically and mentally from being in nature.

What's for dinner? And good night

Bob B's access to food is vast, able to attain food 24 hours a day with little effort, and most of it isn't real food. Eating low nutrient processed foods every few hours leads to energy crashes, hunger and cravings to eat more.

Bob A's food intake would be simple yet nourishing, meat, fish, vegetables, nuts and seeds, fungus and limited seasonal fruit. He would have eaten as and when he could, not three to six times a day.

So how do we fuel our bodies well?

Eat real food in its most natural state; I'm not suggesting you have to hunt it yourself, but base your choice on good quality meat, a wide variety of vegetables, eggs, natural fats from nuts, seeds, avocado, coconut or olives and some fruit in moderation.

Plan your menu for the week, consider where you will be, what's available, do you need to take something with you? Go shopping for everything you need so you're not caught short if you get home late, and stick to the list.

We now come full circle back to sleep; the advice from Good Morning is the same, but also give yourself some relaxation time before trying to settle down, reading, a bath, or perhaps some stretching and breathing routines could also help you.

Conclusion

By having a vision of Bob A's day and using it as a lifestyle template, we can start to eat, move and live the way nature intended. You can't fully replicate his life, and you should appreciate some of the finer things from the modern world. However, I hope you can see how trying to live a more natural lifestyle can significantly improve your health.

CHAPTER 10

The Pathway to Create a Healthy Lifestyle

By Lavinia Milner-Gray

You know what to do; however, you just don't know where to start.

Why, oh why is it so difficult to start? When you do eventually start, why is it so difficult to stick to the steps to create healthy habits?

Developing healthy habits is a challenge for millions of people on the planet. Why is that?

My belief is because it's something we must work at, and we have access to far more junk food than we do healthy food.

Lives have become sedentary for many because their jobs don't require much movement. People have become used to living in their comfort zones, and when it is time to change, it feels uncomfortable and hard.

As I've said countless times, 'change takes time'. Yes, a cliché; however, it is true, 'change does not happen overnight'.

If a healthy, fulfilled, and energetic life is for you, you need to put the effort in. If you want to age gracefully and without every ailment under the sun, then you need to put the effort in.

Many people are misled by the idea that you need to completely overhaul your diet or that you need to smash out hours at the gym every day. You can create a healthy lifestyle by making small changes each day. Where do small changes lead...... you guessed it, big results.

There is an effective path to a healthy lifestyle. The key is simple and effective steps that work for YOU.

There is a plethora of information available at your fingertips, and I totally understand that it gets overwhelming, and before you've even started, you've given up. Anyone who ever tried to change their habits began on a single day. That day turned into a second day, a week, a month, and eventually a year.

There are two key ingredients - persistence and consistency. Starting with a single step today - a short walk each day, more vegetables at each meal or an extra glass of water, will pay off and bring you closer to the healthy body you've always hoped for.

What is YOUR version of a healthy lifestyle?

Once you become clear on what a healthy lifestyle is for you, the following six stepping stones will help you get there. These steps have been tried and tested and have delivered results.

Are you ready? This is where your journey begins…

Fresh Start - Step 1

The first and the most important step in this process is to think of this as a fresh start. This is a chance to create a new chapter in your life. Your chance to curate and cultivate the next phase of your life.

Your chance to distance yourself from all the failed diets and exercise routines and start afresh with what will work.

You have the chance to pause, reflect and think about your future self. How do you envision living the next part of your life?

Adopt a beginner's mind. A fresh new approach to creating a healthy lifestyle.

If it works for you, start on a Monday or the 1st day of a new month. That is when your new chapter will begin.

Katy Milkman's book "How to Change" was a game-changer for me and is now how I approach change.

She investigates and conducts studies on how impactful the thought or opportunity of a fresh start is on someone's motivation to change. During her research, Milkman learned that people thought about their lives in "episodes" rather than perceiving time as a continuum. People create stories from incidents or "chapters" in their lives.

Reflect on your own life, do you reference it in chapters or episodes? Perhaps this strategy will work for you. Embarking on your journey to create a healthier lifestyle is the next chapter in your story.

Knowing your Why - Step 2

Become clear on exactly what you want to change and WHY you want to change your current lifestyle.

Is it to have a healthier diet, feel fitter, have more energy, to have balance and purpose?

Then ask yourself, Why?

Why do I want to be and feel those things?

What is the underlying reason?

You need to move past the surface stuff and get to the core of the reason, the underlying motivation to change your current lifestyle and become the healthiest you can be.

Is it because you have witnessed a family member's ill health, and that has scared you to death? You realise if you keep on the path you are on now, you could be in that position in a year's time.

It could be you are afraid of waking up in ten years' time and realising you have many unfilled dreams because you just didn't have the energy to take action.

Sinek, in "Start with Why", explores how much people can achieve when they start with Why. Once you understand what motivates you, you will succeed in your pursuits. It is a simple yet very powerful concept.

Why are you on this journey to create a healthier lifestyle?

Mini Steps - Step 3

This step gets a little more airtime than the others because we underestimate the power of taking small and consistent actions each day.

Set bite-size goals by making small changes to the area of life you want to change. Accept that change takes time, and no matter what you have been led to believe, change does not happen overnight.

If you want a healthier diet, add one more vegetable to one meal a day and gradually increase your vegetable intake. If you want to become fitter, start with a 10-minute brisk walk, then gradually build on that by adding one more minute to each walk.

Darren Hardy's book "The Compound Effect" solidified for me the fact that small steps do indeed lead to big results. "The Compound Effect is the principle of reaping huge rewards from a series of small, smart choices". Just as you have created habits that no longer serve you, you can use the same concept to change and form habits that are better for your physical and mental wellbeing.

All habits are developed over time; you didn't suddenly wake up one day and all you wanted to eat was two slabs of chocolate.

Over time your body has become accustomed and dependent on high amounts of sugar because it's a learned habit.

The sweet treat now and again became a sweet treat because you were tired, stressed, or you thought you deserved a reward. What would seem an insignificant step, like drinking one more glass of water each day, will over time benefit your health in countless ways. These habits ripple into other areas of life.

The secret sauce is persistence and consistency. When you take persistent and consistent action towards your goal every day, there is only one outcome SUCCESS.

Together We Go Further - Step 4

Create a support network.
Share your goal with a family member or friends who you know will support you, encourage you and keep you accountable (or engage a coach). Everyone needs support and guidance.

As much as we believe we can go it alone, we can get so much further and achieve so much more with the support of a community.

There is a Southern African proverb called 'Ubuntu'. There is no direct translation; however, the philosophy of Ubuntu is "I am because we are".

Its essence is being part of a community and building each other up to better one another and those around us. As much as we would benefit as an individual in achieving our goals, we inspire those around us who, in turn inspire others. This is a ripple effect that has a positive impact on you as well as the people around you.

Imagine a world of healthy, positive, compassionate people. What a wonderful world it would be.

Celebrate - Step 5

Acknowledge and celebrate every change you make and follow through with.

If you drink an extra glass of water or have an extra serving of vegetables, say "well done" to yourself for following through on the commitment you made to yourself and your health.

It is vital to acknowledge oneself for taking action towards your goals. At times during this journey of improving your health or self-development, it is easy to forget what a great effort it has taken to take that one small step each day.

Try not to take yourself for granted. Change is not easy, if it was, we would all be champions at it.

Take a moment each day to say "well done and thank you" to Self for following through on your commitment to improving your life and, in turn, the life of others around you.

Revisit your Why - Step 6

There will be days when it will be tough and you want to fall back into old habits because it's the easy option.

When you are in that place of why am I depriving myself that extra glass of wine or square of chocolate, revisit your WHY. Your reason and your motivation for making this positive change in your life. Your WHY will keep you moving forward.

Approach this new chapter of your life with curiosity and openness. Make it work for you.

You CAN do it.

CHAPTER 11

Health is Holistic

By Lavinia Milner-Gray

As much as you may believe your life is in silos, it is quite frankly all interconnected. It is not surprising that you might believe that diet is separate to sleep, sleep separate to mindset and movement separate to diet.

We must work at being healthy as it is not always something that comes easily. However, when you begin to see and understand the interconnectedness of life, it makes change and creating healthy habits a little easier.

Imagine your health and wellbeing as a four-legged chair. If you took one of those legs away the chair would fall. Your health is similar, if you do not care for each part of your health and wellbeing, then it is unlikely you will succeed in your endeavours.

The concept I am about to introduce you to is not revolutionary. I like to view health as four pillars.

Pillars are often used to describe various aspects of health as it helps you envision your body as a structure. Your structure is strong if all the pillars holding it up are strong. If one pillar is unstable, the entire structure will crumble and fall.

The four pillars of health are mindset, movement, food and sleep. They are all as equally important as the other. The order they are in has no significance except that they roll off the tongue easily.

What has mindset got to do with health?

Your thoughts create your reality.

If you perceive being healthy as too hard, that becomes your belief. Your beliefs influence your mindset. Your mindset influences your level of curiosity.

Curiosity is trying something new, like whether adding more vegetables to your meals will boost your energy. Curiosity is trying a new sport or activity to see if it will improve your fitness and if you enjoy it.

What are you willing to try to help you get that step closer to being in amazing health?

Dr Joe Dispenza puts it eloquently, our 'Cycle of Thinking and Feeling becomes our State of Being'. If you always do what you've always done, you will get more of the same.

A gentle way to begin to shift your mindset is to set an intention each day. Goal setting may not be your thing as it sounds too restrictive, and if you don't follow through, you are consumed with guilt and shame. Intention setting in its gentle way is powerful. Wayne Dyer's "The Power of Intention" had a huge impact on me. When I shifted from goal setting to intention setting, I became more likely to follow through with my "goal". It still works for me today. This practice helped shift my mindset.

I invite you to set an intention today. Drink one more glass of water than you usually would or go outside for a brisk walk. Note how it feels in the body when you set yourself an intention to do one thing to improve your health and wellbeing today. Imagine what your life would be like if you were the healthiest and fittest you could be. What new and amazing opportunities and experiences could you have?

Why is movement essential to your overall physical and mental wellbeing?

Look down at your body and its structure. Your body is made to move and not be sedentary.

Our ancestors moved all the time. If they didn't move, they wouldn't have survived, and you wouldn't be here. Moving meant finding food, shelter and keeping safe.

Unfortunately, our modern lifestyle means that sometimes we don't need to move as much to survive. We can order pretty much anything with a click of a button.

Our bodies need to move, and if we are sedentary for most of our lives, inevitably we become ill both physically and mentally.

Movement is our way of engaging with life. Movement is not only for weight loss. Numerous studies have shown the benefits of movement, including reducing stress and improving memory; it also stimulates creativity and provides clarity.

Movement is joyful, and Kelly McGonigal undertook fascinating research in 'The Joy of Movement', investigating why movement makes us happy and helps prevent inflammation on the brain, which over time helps protect against poor mental health.

Moving our bodies influences our emotions and thoughts.

When you engage in regular movement, your fitness improves and you are more inclined to make healthier food choices.

Regular physical activity also improves your quality of sleep.

Movement is engaging in an activity that is fun, helps you connect with others and motivates you to becoming healthier, happier and more energetic. I invite you to try something you have never tried before like ice skating, swimming, rock climbing, hiking, a dance class or even a brisk walk.

How does the food you eat impact your life?

First, we want to consider food as more than simply fuel.

Food not only impacts your waistline but your mood, emotions, mindset, energy and quality of sleep. Food affects your physical and mental wellbeing. We need food to survive however the quality and quantity of food impacts your quality of life.

There are fascinating studies out there on the link between food and mood. Professor Jacka's 'The Brain Changer' and Ekstedt and Ennart's 'Happy Food' discusses the various studies undertaken on how diet impacts your mental health. When your mental health is impacted, it affects all areas of your life, including decision-making abilities, your cognitive ability and your motivation to exercise.

Your body needs to thrive.

People frequently ask me how they can improve their diet. My response is, add one vegetable to each meal each day and slowly build up your vegetable intake. An effective way to understand how you are feeding your body is to keep a food diary even for just one week. This will help you build awareness around how you are nourishing your body and give you insight into the aspects of your diet you need to tweak. You will begin to tune into your body, experiment and find the foods that will increase your energy, balance your emotions and uplift your mood.

Over time you will improve your diet, and in turn, it will greatly benefit your mindset, your sleep quality, your energy and your motivation to move your body more.

Is sleep underrated?

My resounding answer is YES.

Sleep is totally underrated. You've all heard the maxim, "I'll sleep when I'm dead". Well, if you don't get enough sleep, you will be shortening your life span and speeding up the ageing process. Sleep deprivation has been glorified for years, and those of us who value our sleep have been made to feel like we are lazy because we are not working hard or playing hard every hour of the day.

I'm so pleased that there has been a lot of emphasis on the importance of sleep quality in recent times and the impact it has on our mental and physical wellbeing.

Think about the times when you are sleep deprived, you feel foggy and can't think properly. Your decision-making abilities are impacted. You are either impulsive because you're too exhausted to think, or you don't make a decision at all and miss out on an opportunity.

When you're tired, you are less likely to make healthy food choices and will reach for the highly-processed food in the hope that it will give you the energy boost you so desperately need.

Matthew Walker's 'Why We Sleep' shines the light on the science behind the importance of sleep. He and his fellow scientists have carried out fascinating and insightful research on how sleep enriches your life. As he bluntly says, 'the shorter your sleep, the shorter your life span'.

How can you ensure that you are getting enough good quality sleep each night?

Try a bedtime routine at least five times a week. Practice the regular rhythms of sleep, go to bed and wake up at the same time each day.

Your 'power down hour' is when you are not using any devices. Power down by reading a book, journaling or listening to soft, calming music in a serene and calm environment. Avoid caffeine after midday and alcohol before bed. Try the power down hour and note how you feel over a few days.

I hope you are beginning to see how the four pillars of health are interconnected.

As mentioned, we have been led to believe that various aspects of health and wellbeing are in silos. This is not the case, and hopefully, I have explained how all areas of health and wellbeing are interconnected. Mindset will impact your decision to embark on the journey to improve your overall health. Food will impact your energy which in turn affects your mental health and ultimately your mindset. Movement will impact your mental and physical health, including your sleep quality, and Sleep will impact your overall mental and physical health.

Health is holistic, and how you do one thing is how you do everything. My invitation to you is to become curious, what could you tweak in your current lifestyle to become the healthiest, happiest and fittest you've ever been!

CHAPTER 12

Use Weight to Lose Weight

By Leanne Hawker

So, you think you want to lose weight? Wrong.

No, I definitely want to lose weight.

No, you don't!

I do…

Ok, let's go with that for a minute, I don't want us to get off on the wrong foot.

You've decided to lose weight and start your diet; you do really well and hit your target weight. You feel good! Don't you? Or do you think, 'hmmm maybe I could look better, maybe if I just lose a bit more weight?'

The problem with weight loss is it's all about numbers and targets and less about long term change. I speak to a lot of people who lose weight but still aren't happy with how they look. They've lost the weight they thought they wanted to, but something still isn't right.

That's because most of us don't want to just lose weight, we want to change our bodies.

We want to feel confident when we look in the mirror (which FYI is more about mindset than anything to do with your body), we want to feel good in clothes, we want to have less wobbly bits!

Weight loss will reduce the numbers on the scale but may leave us feeling just as wobbly as we did before, and not only that, every time that number starts to creep up, it sends us into a spin. What does your number actually mean? It tells us nothing about how healthy you are, how much fat you're carrying, how strong you are – it is just the sum of your fat, organs, muscles, water etc., added together! There are lots of 'skinny' people who have quite a high fat percentage. There are quite a lot of 'overweight' people who run marathons! If we think back to diet culture, it's taught us to be obsessed with the numbers because if we all suddenly felt comfortable with ourselves, they would all go bankrupt!

A prime example of what we weigh being a bit of a waste of our focus, is to look at people who body build. If they step on the scales, they weigh a lot; according to the BMI scale, a lot of bodybuilders are classed as obese.

However, this is not accurate as bodybuilders will be carrying a high percentage of muscle mass and a low percentage of body fat. So, not obese at all – which just proves the value of stepping on the scale (and of the BMI scale). Whether you like the bodybuilder look or not, there's no denying that their bodies look lean, taut and clearly muscular.

Keep reading, this is not a how-to on achieving bodybuilder biceps, but it is a guide on how you can adopt some of the principles to achieve the body you want without getting hung up on the scales. It might be scary to start with, as we must overcome the idea of weight being the most important factor in our transformation and start looking at other indicators; such as how our clothes look, how confident we feel when we look in the mirror, does our body look leaner and tighter, are we losing inches even though the weight isn't changing, do we feel mentally better?

Use weight to lose weight! Still with me? If we want to see real body transformation, we need to be adding some weight into our weight loss plan! By this, I mean strength training.

Why strength train over cardiovascular training? Firstly, cardiovascular training is anything that gets the heart rate up, such as running and cycling.

It certainly has a place in our weight loss programmes, especially if you enjoy it, but you can also get a good cardio workout with strength training, particularly through HIIT workouts (High Intensity Interval Training). Diets and cardio training can result in muscle loss, and when we lose muscle, we can slow our ability to burn fat. We want to burn fat, not muscle, in order to achieve the type of physique we really want.

Strength training is anything that involves adding some extra weight or resistance to your workouts. You can use dumbbells, kettlebells, resistance bands, gym machines, tins of beans or your own body weight. (Actually, any tins can be used – I am not being paid by any bean companies!) You will do exercises, such as squats, push-ups, planks, shoulder press, to name a few. Implementing this type of training will help you see real gains in your weight loss goals, even though the scale may show little shift in digits. When you strength train, you will start to see changes to your body shape, such as more definition in your arms, a smaller waist, shapely legs and a firmer butt! I mean, I'm sold already!

The concern most people have, more women than men, is that they will get 'bulky' or too big. I think they usually have an image of some hench bodybuilder in their minds, all glistening pecs and thighs you could break a melon with!

Let me reassure you; these people work hard to achieve these bodies; it takes a lot of dedication, intense meal planning and the willpower of a saint! If this is the sort of look you want, that's OK, and you can do it, but we are really focusing on anyone who wants to feel generally better about their body, with some added strength and 'I can take on the world' attitude thrown in for good measure! (Strength training really can make you feel like a badass, and imagine always being able to open your own wine without help!)

So, what's the secret with this strength training then? You might have heard the phrase 'muscle weighs less than fat', well, of course, that's not true – 5lbs is 5lbs whatever form it comes in.

The difference is that muscle takes up less space than fat; if you have 5lbs of fat vs 5lbs of muscle in your arm, the arm with the muscle will look smaller despite weighing the same. Going back to our bodybuilder from earlier, if they weigh 17 stone and you stand them next to someone else who is 17 stone that doesn't have as much muscle, they will look completely different. The likelihood is that if you had to choose which one you would rather look like, it would be the 17 stone bodybuilder.

When we strength train, we can increase the amount of muscle we have, and there are many benefits to this…

Increased calorie burning! Yay, let's eat all the food! Don't get excited, when we have more muscle, we burn more calories as muscle requires more energy, so you might find you can eat more than when you are on a traditional diet without gaining weight. However, that doesn't mean that you can suddenly start gorging on all the foods! Predominantly, you need to eat foods that fuel your body and feed the muscle, so protein, vegetables, fibre and some carbohydrates, then have the foods you enjoy in moderation.

Increased fat burn! If the increased calorie burn didn't sway you, the next huge benefit to strength training is that you continue to burn calories and fat after your training session! Could this get any better? Even when you're sitting on your butt, those muscles are working away, and the more muscle you have, the more fat you burn.

You will look smaller! When you strength train, you build muscle. Now, remember that muscle takes up less space than fat, so by default, you will look smaller no matter what the scale says; cue smaller dress size incoming!

And let's not forget there are a heap of non-aesthetic reasons for strength training, including increased strength, more functionality; which essentially means you can do actions that most of us take for granted, such as getting in and out of a chair, carrying our shopping etc., and ultimately prolonged independence.

Where to start then? I would suggest finding a professional to help you get your technique right. When starting to strength train this is important in helping to prevent injury, but also to ensure that you get the most out of your workouts and see the results you want. A professional can also help you create a plan that works for you and progresses over time. Trust the process, you won't see a huge change straight away, but if you stay consistent, you will start to see the results you want, and who knows, you might enjoy it too!

CHAPTER 13

It's not me, it's you!

By Leanne Hawker

No one needs to be on a diet... let me say it again louder for the people at the back... NO ONE NEEDS TO BE ON A DIET!

Diets are something constructed by a billion-dollar industry to make us believe we need what they provide to achieve our weight loss goals. Essentially, it keeps making them money, lots and lots of money! I won't lie, I am a bit jealous I didn't think of it myself; I can see myself in the billionaire yacht club! In all seriousness though, if diets worked you wouldn't still be on one.

The reason you are still on one is because the goalposts keep changing – do eat carbs/don't eat carbs; fat is good for you/fat is bad for you; fruit will make you spontaneously combust or maybe not...

The list goes on. Is it any wonder we're all confused, and rather than losing weight, we all seem to be gaining it?

Diets are designed to lead to failure. They very rarely contain any education, or more to the point, the correct education. They make up their own rules about food, and they don't deal with the reason we're gaining weight, which has a lot less to do with food and a whole lot to do with mindset and psychology.

Now don't get me wrong, some people will succeed when following a diet, hitting their target weight and feeling on top of the world. However, for a large percentage of people, once they leave the weekly weigh-in, they will end up gaining the weight back and more. This leads to feelings of failure, and instead of thinking 'maybe there is something wrong with the diet', we automatically think there is something wrong with us. Why can't we stick to it? It worked though because you hit target weight, so off you trot back to the slimming club and do it all again.

Most diets also lead to disordered eating – hands up if you're scared of bread? You're not alone; if I had a £1 for every time someone told me they were avoiding the pretty harmless slice of medium white, I would be in that billionaire club already. How many of you have tried shake meal replacements? Fat burner tablets? Not eating after 6pm? Only eating between certain hours.

How often do you refer to food as good or bad or even worse, refer to yourself as good or bad for eating one of the many items on the forbidden food list? I'm willing to guess you can say yes to a fair few of these, I get it, I've been there too. However, this is not a normal way to think about food, we've just been led to believe it is.

All food is good, whether it's a family-size jar of chocolate spread or a banana. Of course, some foods are more nutritionally valuable than others, but they are all still just food! And the best bit is you don't have to give any of them up – nope, not at all! (You can thank me later).

So, what can you do if you still want to lose weight?

Firstly, break up with that diet today! I don't care if you leave it in the dead of night or go for a face to face break up, but you're getting out of there! As I touched on earlier, dieting ruins our mindset. It sets us up with crazy ideas about food that only lead us to more confusion. It promotes a life of restriction, which ultimately leads to a diet cycle of restrict – crave – binge – guilt – restrict and so on. It leads us down a path of looking for quick fixes, as most diets are designed to get us to lose weight fast.

You'll often see people shouting about the fact they lost 5lbs in the first week of their diet, this leads us to believe the diet plan is working and ties us in.

It also stops us trusting the process of longer weight loss plans because we've been taught that fast results are the answer. (FYI, they are not)!

So, you've broken up with your diet; now you need to start working on that diet mindset. Start by thinking about how you think about food. Have you banished bread from the house or find that you panic if you've eaten after a certain time? Write down anything that stops your enjoyment of food, and then look at whether any of those things have really helped you lose weight. Once you realise how much you've been missing out on for very little gain, you might start to think differently. Now think about your own limiting beliefs around weight loss, what are the stories you tell yourself? For example, 'I never commit to anything', 'I always give up', 'I just can't stop myself eating'.

These limiting beliefs we have about ourselves hold us back in many areas of our lives, and trying to lose weight is no different.

Start reframing those thoughts, 'I can commit to what's important to me', 'I choose to not give up', 'I am in control of what I eat'.

Next, stop standing on the sad step A.K.A the scales! Stay with me, I know it's a lot to take in. Your weight really does not indicate a whole lot about you, and it is certainly not an indicator of success.

Remember when we lost all that weight in week one of our diet? Well, that's because we lost a lot of water, maybe some muscle and possibly a little bit of fat.

Usually on a diet, we will continue to lose muscle, which for a while will show up as a weight-loss, but as muscle really is a great way to burn calories, over time we will find that the weight loss slows down due to the metabolism slowing down. This means only one thing, even less food! The more muscle we keep the better, even if it doesn't seem that way according to the scales. And we will be able to consume more food without putting on weight! Now there's a diet I can get on board with!

Stop fearing foods. No one food is responsible for your weight gain, not even that slice of medium white. Not pasta, not potatoes, not even chocolate or cake. What is responsible is eating too much of these things; eating or drinking too much of anything in fact, even if on the surface it seems healthy.

Having a sandwich at lunch or pasta for dinner is not going to pile on the pounds, remember this is just your diet talking and you broke up. Work on rebuilding your relationship with food again and learning to eat normally.

Stop fearing yourself. Diet culture has us believe that we can't control or trust ourselves around food. This is a lie. If you really couldn't control yourself, wouldn't you gorge on the confectionary aisle whilst in the supermarket?

Or pull over into a layby to eat the shopping before you got it home? You can absolutely control yourself.

Add in before you take away! Think about all the good things you can add to your lifestyle that will aid your weight loss, rather than thinking about all the things you need to remove! Add more fruit and veg to your meals; you want at least half your plate to be vegetables. Add in more protein and make sure you're getting enough fibre. All these changes will leave you feeling fuller and more satisfied. Start drinking more water. Add in some daily movement, yes exercise is important too, but moving about throughout the day can really aid your weight loss and keeps you healthy.

Stay consistent. How many times have you stopped and started your weight loss plan and then decided it doesn't work?

Probably too many to admit to! Unless you stay consistent and give your weight loss plan time to work, you will never hit your goals. Most of the time we struggle to stay consistent because we are trying to do too much at once, so think about making small changes you can stick to, rather than large gestures that go out of the window the minute someone brings cake to the office!

Trust the process! One common theme I see is that people don't trust that a slower, more consistent approach is the answer.

That's because generally speaking, it doesn't produce those quick results we are used to seeing with other diet methods, so it can feel frustrating. Especially when Brenda down the road followed her new diet plan for 2 minutes and lost 2 stone, as she likes to remind you whenever she sees you! What she doesn't tell you is that she cried in the bread aisle and has started licking the outside of chocolate packets. A slower process is sustainable and produces long lasting results, which is generally what we are looking for!

In order to lose weight in an emotionally and physically healthy way, break up with your diet, work on your mindset and stop restricting yourself. Weight loss will just be an added bonus to feeling happier, having a better relationship with food and returning to a life you loved.

CHAPTER 14

Specific Adaptions

By Martin Sharp

Have you ever noticed how each athletes body shape changes depending on the sport they are playing?

Perhaps when watching athletes, you can see the sizeable muscular wedge shape in the great rugby players with wide broad shoulders, muscular arms and legs with narrow hips? Compared to Olympic swimmers who often have long slender bodies, with long arms providing a wider reach and are potentially more flexible and nimble.

Yet have you ever wondered what that difference in body shapes actually means to you?

One of the fundamental and most important concepts in sports science is the SAID principle. Now, SAID stands for Specific Adaptions to Imposed Demand, which means that when the body is placed under some form of stress, it starts to make adaptions that will allow the body to withstand better that stress in the future.

For example, if you want to become a better swimmer, you swim regularly. Each time you practice, your body adapts to strengthen those specific muscles, neural pathways, and other systems by laying down new fibres, replacing damaged cells, etc. The end result is that you get better at exactly what you practice; you may have heard the phrase "practice makes permanent".

This process happens all the time with everything you do and are exposed to because your body is seeking the best way to survive and thrive. It is not just in the now but in the future as well, and it is a vital part of how our ancestors evolved. If you wanted to avoid being lunch to the Sabre-toothed tiger, you had to be a faster runner than the other animals around you.

When you think about your body, you can already find some of these specific adaptions at work. You may find that you prefer to write using your right or your left hand. Because of this favouring of using one side over the other at an early age, then repeating it by practising ever since using that same side, you will probably find that you are more dominant with this hand when it comes to other tasks. Potentially you discover that you have finer motor control and maybe even greater strength with it over your less dominant hand.

If we take an example of tennis players, this dominance of favouring one arm over the other can lead to one arm having larger bones due to the repeated shocks and impacts. Along with thicker and stronger tendons, ligaments and muscles that have developed as a response to the mechanical stress placed upon them, causing them to get bigger.

If you are wondering, "what has this got to do with me?" then think about how you can apply this principle to the goals you have for your body. Do you want to be faster, stronger or endure for longer? Or perhaps you want to lose body fat, develop a more toned look or live a long, happy and healthy life?

It is by understanding that it takes stress to cause adaptions, which keeps you improving and evolving. This is not the bad stress such as mental stress that you get through worry or anxiety without an outlet. When we talk about stress in this context, it is the body's effort in the world in response to its environment.

Drumming your fingers on a table is not going to be enough to strengthen your arm. Likewise, smashing it with a hammer will be too much stress and cause it a problem. Too little stress and there are no adaptions, and too much stress will result in burnout and injury.

Finding the right amount of stress for physical adaptions to occur in your muscular, skeletal and energy systems will result in you getting closer to your goal if these stresses are applied with progressing levels of difficulty. Your goal could be to become bigger, stronger, react faster, etc., or a combination of these, all of which take time and repetition to take effect, whilst at the same time being careful not to get hurt or overtired.

It is not just the adaptions to the physique that occur. There is also a corresponding improvement in motor skills when you practice as the mind to muscle pathways are used. What many people call muscle memory is improving the efficiency (time and speed) of neurons from the brain to muscle, resulting in improvements in hand-eye coordination and reaction times as you start to predict what will happen next

The price your body pays for these adaptions and improvements is an increase in energy usage. Muscle is an expensive resource for your body that takes energy to use and energy to maintain, which means that you need more nutrients to keep it going. When you don't use them, your body looks to become more efficient, breaking down the muscles and therefore no longer needing as much to survive. You may have heard the phrase "use it or lose it".

Suppose we apply the SAID principle to a common weight loss goal that a growing number of people have with the increasing obesity epidemic. In that case, we can use the process of adaption to our advantage.

Weight gain happens when the amount of energy taken into the body through food and drinks is higher than the quantity expended through digestion, exercise, daily movement, and simply being alive. The body is still in a state of adaption at this point, expecting there will be a famine or drought coming up that will cause hardship. Therefore in preparation, it stores the excess as body fat. The explanation of how this specific adaption has come about is through thousands of years of evolution because there wasn't enough food all year round. Those who could last the leaner times through storing energy survived. A clear example of natural selection.

In our modern society, there is no longer a shortage of food; this can lead to overeating compared to the amount of energy used. Even a small surplus will increase weight gain. For example, eating 100 calories more per day than your body requires, the equivalent of 11g of peanut butter (a level teaspoon) or 25g of jam (a slightly heaped tablespoon). Over a week, that is an excess of 700 calories, over a month 3,000 calories and over a year 36,500 calories what starts as seemingly nothing, compounds over time to something significant.

A rule of thumb calculation that some nutritionists use is 1lb (~0.5kg) body fat is equal to 3500 calories, so in the example above, you may be putting on 1lb (~0.5kg) per month, which is around 10.5lb (4.75kg) per year.

A calorie surplus in your life gives you three options to help bring your body back into balance or redress the excess by creating a deficit over a period of time. The first two everyone talks about and are widely known. The first is to reduce the number of calories taken in, and the other is to increase the amount of activity you perform - the often repeated, though not overly helpful, mantra of "eat less and move more". The third option is to make your body more inefficient.

As mentioned above, muscle is an expensive resource for your body because muscle is more metabolically active than body fat, also known as adipose tissue. More metabolically active means using more calories even when at rest to maintain itself.

Therefore, it stands to reason and is backed by scientific studies, that the more muscle you have, the higher the number of calories your body will use. The higher calorie demands that muscles exert explain why many athletes, especially bodybuilders and weight lifters, can and must consume higher than the recommended daily allowance to maintain their ability.

As you can imagine, the process of growing or building muscle is also metabolically demanding, requiring energy and the right nutritional building blocks (such as protein, amino acids and other nutritional elements) to be in place. When these are in place, and the right stimulus is applied, such as resistance training, adaptions start to take effect. These adaptions come as a response to the stress caused to the muscle, the damage (or injury), through use, which the body responds to by repairing and increasing the mass and size.

If you have ever had a cut that has left a scar, this is a similar process. You may notice that the scar line is still visible, potentially the skin is thicker or harder as well, where your body has made the repair compared to the surrounding skin.

Also, the process is not instantaneous. Just like when you have had a cut, it takes a few days to heal, the same with building your muscles. They require more energy and building blocks even after the stimulus has finished, which means that the resistance training session will be having an effect over the following days as well.

By setting out your personal goals for your own body and thinking about the specific adaptions it will need to achieve them, you can set out a plan of action for providing the right stimulus and environment to give yourself the best chance of achieving them.

CHAPTER 15

Non-negotiables

By Martin Sharp

Would you be willing to tell a white lie to save someone's feelings?

Or would you be inclined to lie to get your way?

Or do you tell the truth all the time?

What about taking something that you weren't sure you had permission to?

Or where do you stand on outright theft?

We all live by our own values, moral code or principles; call it what you will. These often unconscious rules define what you will and won't accept from others, also what you will and won't accept from yourself.

Your values are not about the to-do list or things you think you should do or believe other people expect of you, like not working on weekends, promising yourself a weekly massage, exercising each day, meditating, etc. Your real values, your core values, are the deep down feelings that drive you, the ones that get you out of bed every day and make you do what you do.

If you are thinking, "Hang on, isn't this a health book? Why are we talking about values?" then it is worth reflecting on the relationships between your feelings, thoughts and behaviours. When talking about health, many will jump straight to the action.

As in how you can modify your behaviours so you can lose weight, gain muscle, become fitter, stronger, healthier. Possibly by introducing more incidental movement in your day by increasing the number of steps, so you perform 10,000 or more, taking the steps rather than the elevator or cycling to work rather than driving. The increase in activity may potentially include deliberate and targeted actions by bringing in some formal resistance, cardio or team sport based exercise. And maybe even addressing what they are eating, choosing healthier options, taking care of portion control and looking at their nutrient balance.

Yet, how long do these actions really last? It feels like there are stories wherever you look about people who have the best intention to do what is right for themselves and put themselves into action, only to come to a screeching halt moments later.

The classic example of this is the New Year's resolution, probably one of the biggest sales days for gym and diet club memberships.

If you are a regular gym user, you've probably witnessed this first hand as it is hard to get onto equipment in January due to the crowds of people determined to make a difference in their lives. Only to find that in February, the tumbleweeds have returned, and you can get back on with your own workout in peace and without delays or having to find alternatives to the exercise you want to perform.

The reason why this happens is that something else in their life becomes more important. It could be anything from a new project at work, wanting to spend more time with their kids, or simply wanting to watch a couple more hours of TV. These hold a higher value in their life and come higher in their thoughts and feelings, resulting in a change of behaviour.

This change of action may be regressing to their previous behaviour, which they wanted to move away from because it may be causing them difficulty, upset or other problems. However, the pain of changing and adopting a healthier lifestyle is perceived as more significant than staying where they are, no matter how much action they take.

As such, just taking action alone is not enough to create sustainable change; it has to be backed by thoughts and feelings for the change to come into effect, be lasting and ultimately provide the outcome you are looking for.

The trio of thoughts, feelings and behaviours control most of our automatic responses and influence our conscious or intentional responses. They are not independent of one another either and exert a significant influence on how each one responds.

- Emotions influence our thoughts – have you ever felt down and had dark thoughts?
- Thoughts influence our behaviour and actions – have you ever thought of something and then immediately had to write it down?
- Actions and behaviour influence our emotions – have you ever felt elated when you have won a sporting event, beaten your personal best or just finished a good session at the gym or hill walking or cycling?
- Emotions influence our actions and behaviour – have you ever been sad and reached for chocolate or other comfort food?
- Action and behaviour influence our thoughts – have you ever had a great idea when you have been out for a walk or a run?
- Thoughts influence our emotions – have you ever had a memory that has made you smile or laugh out loud?

It is all well and good knowing this and agreeing how it logically fits together, yet the thing is, we don't always act logically or rationally! Many of our responses are instinctive, governed by our autonomous mind like an autopilot. Some people have described this as the monkey or reptilian mind or the freeze, fight or flight response. That part of us that that requires no effort. It's fast and takes care of most situations based on previous experience and habits we have formed.

Without this part of us, we would be overwhelmed every minute of the day; consider the sheer volume of information your body takes in each moment, from your eyes, ears, taste buds, smell receptors, nerve endings, etc. It is also error-prone, and it can prejudge people and events, leading to prejudice and succumbing to stereotyping and poor responses.

The thing is, for some, their own health becomes a casualty, as everything else becomes the priority either out of habit and learned behaviour or instinct because they don't have the values to interrupt the pattern.

When you clearly understand what you value the most, you can lend this value to your own personal change, as in you cannot live by your values unless you change.

These need to be your highest values because there are many things you will value in your life, though it is only the top three that you will act on at any cost, the non-negotiables.

As an example, if you take a look at my own transformation. When I examined my values, the top three became very clear:

- I love my family. I want them to grow up with wonder and curiosity and to positively contribute back into the world with love and happiness in their hearts, knowing that they have a good grounding and support.
- I support my friends and enjoy spending time with them. They enrich my life, and I aim to enrich theirs.
- I serve my clients as I want them to succeed in the ventures they are undertaking. I go beyond what is expected and do so gladly, so they get what they need as well as what they want.

All this came at a cost, though, to my own health as I put my family, friends and clients ahead of my well-being, especially when I started up my own business. This cost manifested itself in an expanding waistline from 34" to 54". My weight increased from 88kg (194lb or 13 stone 12lb) to 154kg (340lb or 24 ¼ stone), and then there was the pain, especially in my back, and problems with movement.

By applying my top three values to my own transformation, it became easy to realise that my behaviour was contrary to those values and something needed to change. I was putting other people before myself. This poor prioritisation was decreasing my self-care and well-being, decreasing my movement, increasing my stress levels, decreasing quality sleep, rest and recovery periods, all while making food sporadic and to what was available quickly in the moment.

When examining this with my core values, I saw that if I had continued on this path, then eventually, I would no longer be able to support my family, friends and clients. In fact, I may become a burden to them as I may become so ill they would need to take care of me!

This simple realisation and alignment changed my thoughts and emotions, resulting in me making time for myself, eliminating some of the stresses in my life (people, actions or things), and guiding my decisions. It didn't mean I couldn't do what I did before. I still love my family, support my friends and serve my clients. However, it did mean that changes occurred. The big ones like exercising regularly and eating mindfully, as you would expect.

Also, more minor changes like no longer drinking alcohol at business functions because it is the done thing.

Saying no to taking on more responsibility because it seems no one else will and making others pick up some of the tasks. And a multitude of others that were contributing like death by thousand cuts.

Are you going to find time now to understand what genuinely are your core values, those that get you out of bed every day and drive you to do what you do?

When you do, you may have just unlocked the key to making your next transformation a success.

CHAPTER 16

Tapping into our Emotional Health

By Ramona Stronach

Our relationship with our emotions

How do you look after your emotional health? What do you do when those uncomfortable, painful feelings and subtle or intense bodily sensations arise and claw at you over and over?

Do you discard them, stuff them deep down within, and fear them? Many of us were never taught how to connect to our feelings. Yet it is critical for our physical and mental well-being if we are to create the lives we desire in our hearts.

We can go a day, a week, a month and so on and not tune in to how we really feel. But what if our feelings and body sensations are talking to us? We may have learned to regard our feelings as if they are something to be apprehensive about, feared even.

Yet how we process our emotions is key to how we live our potential as human beings.

However, unless we were raised by conscious care takers who were in touch with their emotions and were able to nurture us through our emotional teething difficulties as babies and children, many of us deal with our emotions in ways that do not serve us.

This is evident just by observing our very own behaviours, that of our closest circle and people in our community and beyond in our world. The lack of honouring our own feelings, not taking full responsibility for them, and the fact that so many of us are actually disconnected from our bodies, shows up by making choices that do not serve us in life, blame, addictions, dis-ease and even violence.

When I first learned it takes 90 seconds for an emotion to pass through the body, I was astounded. I had always felt I was at the mercy of my emotions, feeling like I was a very tiny wooden boat being thrashed around in a torrent of painful emotional seas at uncountable times in my life. I have no doubt many of you can relate to this. I thought that my feelings were always in control.

I didn't really know how to relate to my emotions, how to acknowledge, accept and unravel their meaning for me.

Then I met the Emotional Freedom Technique (EFT), or tapping as it is more commonly known, which is tapping on the end of meridian points on parts of the body to move energy through our system. Picture acupuncture without needles. I learnt how to start having "cards on the table" chats with my emotions.

It facilitated a deeper and healing relationship with my emotional body and has opened so much possibility for me that I thought I could never attain because of my own limiting beliefs, some of which were conscious, many not.

What happens when we do not take care of our emotional health?

Emotions are energy in motion, and when energy in our bodies cannot flow freely, it becomes stuck. If we keep stuffing down feelings we don't like, if we do not allow ourselves to feel them and therefore flow through our body system, we risk energy blockages. Our bodies respond by trying to get our attention to warn us, and if we continue to suppress emotions, the result can show up in the mental and physical body and in our personal energy field. We can experience low moods and ill mental health. We can feel energy loss, develop physical symptoms in the body and eventually, the body may try to get our attention by developing dis-ease.

We may experience a lack of flow in life, and our external world mirrors our internal state in a less than satisfactory way. We can end up attracting the opposite of what we want in our life.

Our emotional body is like an amazing message system. When we experience an unpleasant feeling, it is the body's intelligence communicating with us.

For example, somebody wants something from you but don't get a great feeling (the body's message something isn't right.). You dismiss the feeling (putting others' needs that do not feel right before your own) and go along with it for fear of hurting their feelings (being out of attunement with your feelings). Next time you experience this, observe how you feel. It will likely be a contracted sensation because you haven't paid attention to your body's message.

If you don't back your feelings up with the right action for you, you could experience continued discomfort. You may berate yourself; your self-talk is probably along the lines of 'should' have done this or that. You may have other feelings arise that cause discomfort. You may choose to continue to ignore your feelings. But your subconscious and your body do not forget.

When we feel an emotional charge in our body, it has a message for us.

Something in our energy field has not been resolved from our past. Otherwise there would be no intensity.

Often these sensations link back to an earlier time in our lives where our body's physiological response (the fight-flight mechanism preparing us to run from danger) to a real or perceived threat (trauma) kicked in, and we experienced emotional intensity. When we are triggered, the body is remembering this past trauma as if it was happening in the now.

When we repeatedly experience emotional intensity over and over, the natural physiological stress response is triggered. The problem is that in modern daily life, we are often not conscious we are stressed until our body starts to give us the smoke signal. Prolonged stress has become the background wallpaper for many of us, but this is not our natural state to be in as humans.

Emotions and beliefs

Let's look at how beliefs can cause us stress. Our core beliefs are formed in our subconscious based on our perception of our experiences between 0 and 6 years of age. Our perceptions are influenced by parents or caregivers, our wider environment, schooling, societal and cultural belief systems, including the mainstream narratives of the time.

If the beliefs are not ones that serve us in life, they can create havoc on our life choices and health.

If we have predominantly positive experiences during these early years, it is likely we will have better serving beliefs and make better choices for ourselves as adults. The thing with our core beliefs is that as they are formed in the subconscious; we are not always aware of how they are impacting us, and we often wonder why we end up in the same old rut, over and over again.

How do our beliefs shape our emotions? Let us look at the belief that many of us have been influenced by, that it is selfish to put our own self-care needs first. Even though we may feel exhausted and run down, because we have made an arrangement with someone, we go against our feelings and continue the plans, feeling guilty if we cancel. But then we run the risk of feeling resentment. If we keep on saying yes because we believe it is selfish to put ourselves first, we end up spilling our resentment energies out into our lives. This can show up as passive-aggressiveness, control issues and projection onto the outer world. Or our bodies start to respond in ways that actually protect us, such as a cold to force us to rest, even though we may not recognise this.

Worse still, life gives us more situations to become resentful because the Law of Life is "like attracts like". Then we run the risk of looking outside of ourselves to distract us because we ignore how we feel.

The distraction from ourSELF

We live within a reality where distraction from who we really are, our deepest Self, is the name of the game. We no longer seem to trust our own true voice, yet we are willing to trust external agencies or authorities. We have many voices, but it is our feelings that, I believe, point us to our true voice; they never lie to us. The Self knows the truth in any moment. And when we go against our Self, I believe this is where our personal suffering arises.

Non-acceptance of how we feel is like a dam. It blocks the energy from flowing through our body systems. We become in resistance mode, and this can range from an unpleasant to a painful feeling. In this state, we find it challenging to move forward in our lives. Life seems to be a struggle. Or we may think we are doing OK, going through the functions of life, but when we don't have a relationship with our Self, we function in lower vibrational energies, and our lived experience is at the opposite end of being tuned into doing what we love.

We lose touch with our fully creative, materialising, actualising Self that raises the vibration here on our stunning planet and beams out to everyone in our sphere and beyond because we are connected by energy.

So when we resist our feelings, we are more vulnerable for the external world (anything and everything outside of ourselves; outside our own physicality, outside of our own minds) to pull our attention away from our inner state, and we can end up doing things automatically that do not serve us in a wholesome and healthy way. Or going along with what everyone else is doing because it is too uncomfortable to listen to our feelings, despite a deep inner knowing that something isn't right.

To listen within can be extremely challenging because it can be just too painful to do so. Because of this, the dependency upon the external world to distract us from our pain becomes attractive. When we are not emotionally healthy, it is all too easy to become hooked on something - whether that is news, violence, consumerism, food addictions, unhealthy sexual addictions, alcohol addictions, social media, drama addictions, the narrative of the day etc. Being hooked on something is not being in balance with our own nature. So when we are not in a state of emotional balance, we are at risk of making decisions that are not right for us; that do not make us feel expansive and feel aliveness.

We actually become disconnected from critically thinking too. When we are not in a state of equilibrium with our emotional health, we forget who we really are, beyond our ego. So the external can distract us away from the consciousness aspect of our true nature, the power to create our life, to heal ourselves.

Therefore, we must reclaim our relationship with our emotional body to find our own truths in life. To learn to be in relationship with our feelings and understand the connection between what we think and feel. We must have courage to have a relationship with painful and uncomfortable emotions if we want to live our best lives in accordance with our potential, our desires and dreams of how we want to show up in this life.

How do we take good care of our emotional health?

Awareness is critical. It is the pause that cracks open a space to listen within and, therefore, space for attunement, even if the pause is tiny. It takes practice, but it becomes easier the more we use our awareness muscle. To take good care of our emotional health is to be in attunement to how we feel in any given moment, acknowledging it and accepting how we feel. It is about not ignoring or suppressing our feelings no matter how uncomfortable or painful they are. Think about the emotional attunement you have to someone you love.

You wouldn't ignore their feelings or yell at them for having their feelings, would you? You would take the time to ask how you could support them. You would be there for them. So it is the same principle with your feelings.

Supporting our feelings is taking the right action for ourselves. When you take action that resonates for you, you back yourself up, and you will likely experience an expansive feeling, a sense of release/relief that feels good.

I now picture my emotional body as a best friend, as I find this perception helpful to support myself, particularly after a meltdown, an upsetting event, a painful memory that still holds intensity, or if I find I am in resistance to a feeling or situation, which in essence is resistance to the present moment.

I never understood the connection between emotions and health. I thought I had no control over my emotions and that I was doomed to always feel a certain way or be at the mercy of them, and tapping turned this around. Once we understand that the emotional intensity is trapped energy, we can empower ourselves more. The emotional intensity no longer has power over us.

When I tap, I have a conversation with the intensity, first of all acknowledging its presence as I would a friend's emotional distress. Tapping enables me to look at whatever is triggering me from a more centred space. And why is this important? When the emotional intensity grip loosens, the fight-flight response becomes less active and we experience more calm.

We are telling our body that we are safe; it is OK to feel what we feel. This then reduces the risk of the stress response chemical cortisol searing around our body, threatening to cause harm to our immune system. If we experience repeated episodes of emotional intensity, we are at risk of prolonging the state of fight or flight, and this can severely impact our immune system and our health.

When I tap, I literally experience freedom from the emotional charges I feel.

Now, this doesn't mean to say I do not feel emotional pain or will never experience painful feelings again over something else in life. It means the time experiencing the intensity becomes less. It means that I can meet emotional pain with more compassion, an inner space opens up within, and I find that what happens is a different perception of whatever is causing the emotional pain arises. I am in touch with that wise part of my Self that is all-knowing.

Further to this, the deepening of my relationship with my emotions through tapping has brought about natural and spontaneous openings to forgive myself as clarity of situations has arisen. This has brought me relief and freed me from the stuck, heavy and painful energy of blame – emotional freedom at its best.

Practising the art of accepting our whole selves

Most of us have never been taught to accept ourselves in the moment of whatever arises emotionally.

It is incredibly challenging to accept ourselves if we dislike aspects of ourselves, live with physical pain daily, have health issues, depend on others for our care needs, dislike another or feel angry or not good enough etc. However, if you cannot accept how you feel, you cannot move forward. Energy becomes stuck. Resistance to accepting ourselves blocks us even more from being free from painful emotions.

When we get to the bottom of why we feel how we feel, it is truly liberating. Tapping can help us to have that conversation with ourselves to dig deep. It does however, take a degree of honesty. Who wants to admit that their behaviours have been unsavoury? That is just an open invite for shame to walk right in! And shame needs to be buried, doesn't it? Isn't that the subliminal message we were told as children?

Tapping gives us a safe space to really accept ourselves, including painful emotions like shame. It gives us permission to say even though we feel this or did something that wasn't great, we accept how we feel, we accept the situation and love ourselves unconditionally anyway.

We have many aspects to us, and often we try and suppress those we don't particularly love and many of us of find it very challenging to love ourselves. But with tapping, we meet ourselves wherever we are.

We can choose instead to accept we are a great person, or choose to be kinder to ourselves when we tap. In tapping, we explore these lower energy emotions and get curious as to why we feel them; what happened? What is the belief behind what happened? Whose belief have you been carrying? Is that belief really true etc.?

It enables us to connect dots in our lives and assure us that we are OK no matter what has happened to us, what is going on around us or within us. And that is truly liberating.

Abundant health and well-being is energy flowing

Life is a constant flow of energy. It is our job to caretake and be responsible for our own energy flow. When our emotions (energy in motion) are turbulent, our health suffers.

We need to honour our emotions, witness them and give them a safe space to reveal themselves and their wisdom to us. This is the connection to emotional freedom. When we are internally free from any extreme emotional intensity, our physical body is happy. Our mental body is happy. We make fulfilling life choices daily. We start to understand that we do not need to be dependent on anything outside of ourselves to make us happy and that this depletes our power.

When we allow ourselves to be with our emotions through tapping, we enable energy to flow freely.

We spend less time in reaction mode to the external, which can only be good for our health, our loved ones around us and the collective consciousness. When we take responsibility for how we feel, we begin to open up to healing on all levels, and when we clear our energy, we open up to all that is possible for us.

CHAPTER 17

Laugh Yourself Healthy

By Sofia Nordgren

A healthy lifestyle is important and we have become noticeably more aware of this, especially during the Covid pandemic that has affected us all in different ways. I would love to inspire you to be more in charge of your own health.

Move more towards "Laugh yourself healthy instead of living in a dead time". This is a short introduction to reaching holistic and sustainable health. It will be a small taste of Sofia's Life + health recipe.

Imagine a beautifully polished vehicle shining in the sun. Then you test drive it and are a little disappointed when you realise it drives sluggishly and squeaks when you have to brake. Or sometimes it can be the other way around, the hood is unpolished, dirty, but it may be fast when you drive it. There are many different small engine parts under the hood that interact in different ways; if some are missing, broken, or the wrong model, the result will be completely different.

You do not know how it works if it will last and run well for two weeks, two years, or 20 years.

How often do you inspect the car? Once a year, after three years? Do different parts need to be replaced? Are some parts rusty? Are you aware of the various signs of when to replace a particular part and that it must be the right part for the car model otherwise there can be fatal consequences? There can be different cost consequences depending on whether or when you pay heed or ignore the signals that something is starting to get worn out. It is important to think about what fuel you add to your car or your body.

A human body can, in some ways, be compared to a car. How we look on the outside does not always have an obvious parallel with how the internal organs (engine) look and how they work together. We also have different DNA and body shapes that affect the result. One person may be slim and not put much focus on keeping the weight off. In contrast, other people have tried different diets and occasionally exercised without reaching their ideal weight.

Several other things also come into play, how we feel mentally, emotionally and spiritually. What does our nuclear family look like, family, friends; what support have we received in various adversities? How do we handle different challenges?

How we feel emotionally affects our internal organs and manifests itself in different ways sooner or later.

How you listen to your body, how you act and understand what to do to feel better is essential too. Perhaps you're over-anxious, a hypochondriac who maybe magnifies every little hassle. On the other extreme, for example, maybe you have a sore knee, having trained hard and intensively for an extended period on hard surfaces in unsuitable shoes. You ignore the symptoms, resulting in you needing an operation on the knee and a long rehabilitation.

It is also essential to know who to turn to. Which expert in which area. Some things sound obvious; for example, I go to the hairdresser if I want a haircut. And if I have a toothache, have rashes, or something else, I do not hire a gardener! When we face a long-term challenge, and one visit to one doctor will not be enough, you need to find the right specialist in the correct field.

How does your inner body, mind, emotions, and soul feel, and how do they function together?
It is important to do regular detox and internal cleansing and cleaning. There are different methods. It's like cleaning at home, and it's up to you how often, when and with what methods you clean.

Is it enough just to brush the floor, vacuum, dry the floor, dust, or you should do a deep cleaning?

Are there some rooms, closets with closed doors, storage, basement space that you have not had time to clean for a while? They may have accumulated layer upon layer of dust and dirt over the years.

A comparison can be made with our minds, with previously hidden traumas and unresolved emotional experiences that are hidden. We do not want to see or feel them. The same applies to our inner body, organs and health. Most things will catch up with us sooner or later.

Many of us struggle to achieve different goals; whether it is our health, sports goals, or something different, we often have challenges with maintaining motivation. We get an idea, a thought about how we want to achieve a goal, or we are inspired by someone else who has achieved something that we also want to achieve. Motivation is something that does not happen all the time; it can disappear, become weaker in certain periods.

We can talk about wanting to achieve this goal for ourselves, but having the motivation to perform the task, is entirely different.

Today there is a lot of information out there on social media, various books and movies. There is no lack of knowledge. We need the right knowledge, coach, mentor and a realistic time frame to implement and achieve new different goals.

It can be challenging to create a new habit. It's OK to fall and get back up again. Motivation is not something you can buy on a shelf in the store with an expiration date!

Do you feel healthy, energetic, motivated and full of passion?

Or?

Have you been feeling ill, waking up tired in the morning, wanting to sleep a little longer, feeling stressed, lost your energy, motivation and passion? You might be experiencing some of these or know somebody close to you who is. How can you find a balance between your work, your personal life, family life and the expectations of others?

It's vital to take care and prioritise yourself first. Just like when we fly, the flight attendant announces that should there be an emergency, we should always put on our life jackets first before we help other passengers and children around us. This means that we must prioritise and put our health first. It is perhaps easier said than done in practice.

I will now share more about me, my background, and how I created a system for reaching more holistic and sustainable health. I love to help you to "laugh yourself healthy instead of living in a dead time"!

My name is Sofia Nordgren, and I live in Stockholm, Sweden however, I was born in Bangladesh. When I was three years old, I sat on the plane without my parents to travel across half the globe to start a new life chapter in Sweden. I was adopted and moved to a small village outside Ludvika in Dalarna. I had a challenging childhood with a lot of fights in the family. In school, I experienced a lot of bullying in my early years. I started to write a diary about my experience, I wanted to share it with others, but I was a little shy in my early childhood.

In 9th grade, at our graduation, I stood on the stage and read my own poem. I enjoyed it, and it went well and was appreciated. I sang as well with some other girls. As a child, I had dreams of standing on the stage doing public speaking. I heard about the possibility of going to the United States as an exchange student and a glimmer of hope was ignited; I would have the opportunity to experience something different. I raised money to be able to complete the trip, and once there, I gave my first international lecture sharing about Swedish culture and traditions.

Back home in Sweden, I studied to become a registered nurse. After working as a registered nurse visiting different workplaces in Sweden during my 25 years within the health industry, I saw many work environments that were very stressful.

They had inefficient routines, and staff were often sick, with low energy, low motivation, and a lack of passion.

I also noticed that all the advice we gave patients lacked "preventative care". This had many negative effects, and I felt frustrated to be part of this unhealthy environment.

After working in this environment, I became sick, close to burned out, found it difficult to sleep, difficult to focus, and I had anxiety. I went to the healthcare clinic and asked for help. The doctor "signed me off" sick for some weeks, but they did not have any special advice on how I could get back on track.

This was a turning point for me; I investigated how I could educate and impact companies with a more holistic and sustainable health approach. I started to educate myself more within the health sector and took several health, personal development, leadership, and business courses. I travelled to India and did several courses and meditation at a meditation centre.

I took a public speaking course in London. I become a Zumba instructor, a passion test coach and a stand-up comedian.

Then I created my own healthcare formula to help companies, staff, managers, and entrepreneurs reach more sustainable and holistic health, using my preventing care toolbox of inspirational speech, individual coaching, and digital videos.

Combining the holistic approach with both Eastern and Western knowledge and a touch of stand-up comedy, I developed my success formula, which I call Life +.

Now I am a CEO, Founder of Life +, Motivational speaker, host, Co-author, coach and a stand-up comedian!

I've been a host/moderator in the City Hall (where the Nobel prize is held), an international speaker, a stand-up comedian (Berlin, New York and in Sweden), a dancer, been in Swedish TV shows and movies, done radio interviews, been in a few books as a co-author, writing some articles and been published in different magazines such as Huffington Post, Women Entrepreneur, Svensk Damtidning.

Here is my formula for reaching holistic and sustainable health, which I call Life +.
1. Good nutrition, food,

2. Diet

3. Strengthen the immune system

4. Good Sleep

5. Rest, recovery, meditation, own time

6. Regular exercise

7. Motivation, positive mind-set

8. Balance between work and leisure time

9. Good energy, energy management, increase energy

10. Embrace your passion, dreams, find and create your pathway.

11. Good scheduling, time management

12. Stress management

13. Have fun, the positive impact of laughter

14. Surround yourself with the right positive and supportive people

15. Good Communication

16. The importance of breathing

17. Detox, inner cleanse

18. Handle Corona pandemic, isolation.

19. Stay up to date, knowledge, courses.

20. Hire a coach, mentor

Start the day with a healthy tea, celery juice, or a smoothie.

- Ginger counteracts inflammation, nausea, osteoarthritis and sore muscles, lowers your blood pressure and strengthens your immune system

- Garlic stimulate the immune system, antibacterial
- Lemon strengthens your immune system, balances the pH value in the body, cleanses your body of toxins, reduces your cravings for sweets, boosts your mood, helps with digestion
- Turmeric improves digestion, functionality in joints, regulation of blood sugar, Improve liver function, improves blood circulation, strengthens the immune system, counteracts inflammation, improves brain function
- Cinnamon is full of antioxidants that play an important role in our health by protecting against free radicals, fight infections, and help with diabetes as it can lower blood sugar and has a positive effect on insulin sensitivity.
- Celery juice contains Vitamins A, B, C, E, Folic acid and the minerals potassium, sodium, calcium, zinc, magnesium, iron, sulphur, phosphorous, copper, silica. It has an anti-inflammatory effect, helps improve digestion and can cure, among other things, IBS, migraines, high blood pressure, allergies and various autoimmune diseases

Sleep:
- 25% of us have sleep deprivation
- and 10% have severe sleep problems

Some symptoms of sleep deprivation/sleep problems are:

- Fatigue
- Difficulty concentrating
- Poor memory
- Burnout
- Depression
- Impaired reactivity
- High BT
- Impaired "repair capacity"
- Immune system compromised
- Recurrent infections
- Abdominal obesity
- risk of diabetes 2
- heart problems

The good effects of sleep:

- The brain receives new energy
- Memory increases / strengthens
- The immune system is strengthened

Ways to improve your sleep:

- Avoid alcohol, coffee, energy drinks
- Read a book
- Drink soothing tea
- Meditation

- Listen to relaxing, calm music
- Shower or take a bath before going to bed
- Avoid social media tv, FB, mobile 1 hour before bedtime
- Regular training
- Mute your mobile phone
- Ensure your bedroom is quiet, dark, and cool
- Unwind 2 hours before bedtime
- Avoid any physical activity late in the evening
- Turn the clock away
- Sing
- Get some CBT (Cognitive Behavioural Therapy)
- Do not go to bed hungry but don't eat too late
- Have a regular bedtime routine
- Do some relaxation exercises
- Avoid too much activity, events, people before bedtime
- Go to bed before midnight as you'll get more good quality sleep

Ways to Increase your energy management:
Here are some suggestions to stimulate many feel-good hormones such as cortisol, oxytocin, serotonin and dopamine.
- dance
- play music
- laugh
- massage

- sex
- sing
- hugs
- eat chocolate
- be with good friends, family
- Read a book
- Watch a feel-good movie

Get some rest and "alone time"

Statistics say that 80% of us experience some kind of stress at work, and 40% experience a lot of stress.

It is so important to rest, slow down and take some downtime by yourself. Listen to your inner voice; having too many expectations from your family, manager or yourself for an extended period can result in tiredness, being unfocused or exhaustion.

We are all affected differently by the opinions of others.

Here are some activities for keeping yourself grounded, focused and relaxed:

- Meditate every morning for at least 10 minutes
- Go for a walk alone for at least 30-60 min
- Listen to relaxing meditation music for 15-30 min.

- Practice nose breathing for a few minutes; it can help improve oxygen circulation in your body
- Get a massage; it relaxes your inner and outer body.
- Set clear boundaries
- Evaluate how much time you spend on social media, TV and practice time management.

I hope these insights give you the impetus to take charge of your own health step by step towards a lasting holistic and sustainable health where you can Laugh yourself healthy instead of living in a dead time.

EPILOGUE

Thank you for purchasing a copy of this book.

I hope you were able to find some answers to your own situation or take some knowledge away to use in your own life. Health should be our number one priority as it allows us to do everything else we love to do.

The Authors within these pages have dedicated their career to finding the answers on areas they are passionate about.

All of our Authors share their own knowledge and experience here and it is their own opinions which are written.

If you would like to share your own experience, please do contact us for details on how you can take part in our next book.

If you enjoyed this book, we would love a review on Amazon.

REFERENCES / BIBLIOGRAPHY

Chapter 4

* Cornell University/Newswise **Kelly McGonigal in The Willpower Instinct

Chapter 10

Milkman, K. (2021). How to Change. 1st ed. London: Penguin

Sinek, S. (2009). Start with Why. 1st ed. USA: Penguin

Hardy, D. (2020). The Compound Effect Jumpstart Your Income, Your Life, Your Success. 3rd ed. New York: Hachette

Paulson, S. (2020). I Am Because We Are: The African Philosophy of Ubuntu. [online] Available from:

https://www.ttbook.org/interview/i-am-because-we-are-african-philosophy-ubuntu

Chapter 11

Dispenza, J. (2012). Breaking the Habit of Being Yourself. 1st ed. London: Hay House UK

Dyer, W. (2004). The Power of Intention. 1st ed. Carlsbad. Hay House Inc.

McGonigal, K. (2019). The Joy of Movement. 1st ed. New York. Penguin Random House

Jacka, F. (2019). Brain Changer. 1st ed. Australia. Macmillan

Ekstedt, N and Ennart, H. (2017). Happy Food. 1st ed. Sweden. Bookmark Forlag

Walker, M (2017). Why We Sleep. 1st ed. USA. Penguin Books

Chapter 16

Karl Dawson, Sasha Allenby, Matrix Reimprinting using EFT, 2010

Shakti Gawain, Living in the Light, 1998

Sir David Hawkins, The Map of Consciousness Explained, 2020

Bruce Lipton, The Biology of Belief, 2005

Jill Bolte Taylor, My stroke of Insight: a Brain Scientist's Personal Journey, 2005

Eckhart Tolle, A New Earth 2005

ABOUT THE BOOK CREATOR

Sharon Brown moved to the West Midlands in 2003 from Glasgow in Scotland. After a wide-ranging career in Event Management, Marketing, Project Management and board level support in various different industries, Sharon's passion around organising events led her to launch Lydian Events Ltd in 2015 whilst still working full time.

In 2017 Sharon took the plunge and left her corporate position to move into Self-employment full time. It wasn't long after this that Sharon soon realised the way business was heading and decided to launch an online platform for women in business in 2018 called Revival Sanctuary with the aim of connecting women globally in order to find collaborative projects to work together and build each other up.

In 2021, Sharon changed the name of her business to Lydian Group Ltd which supports four online platforms. She has now found a real passion for helping small business owners avoid the mistakes she made by raising their profiles through writing, speaking, publishing and community opportunities.

SERVICES

MO2VATE Magazine | The Winning Formula

mo2vatemagazine.com | editor@mo2vatemagazine.com

A global publication which highlights the writing ability and knowledge around business, health and inspirational stories of small business owners the world over.

———

THE BOOK CHIEF | Ignite Your Writing

Thebookchief.com | sharon@thebookchief.com

An affordable and full service to get your manuscript edited, typeset and published through a recognised brand with a niche in collaborative books.

———

THE SPEAKERS INDEX | Amplify Your Voice

Thespeakersindex.com | sharon@thespeakersindex.com

A speakers and event organiser directory and magazine to allow you to get in front of the right people.

———

REVIVAL SANCTUARY | Women in business

Revivalsanctuary.co.uk | sharon@revivalsanctuary.co.uk

Exclusive Private Membership Club for women in business. It attracts women who are comfortable in their own skin, supportive of other women and those willing to empower and collaborate with each other.

———